Assessment Program

OXFORD PICTURE DICTIONARY

SECOND EDITION

Christine Griffith, Susan Iannuzzi,
Christina Kubes, Andrew London, and Alisa Takeuchi

OXFORD
UNIVERSITY PRESS

198 Madison Avenue
New York, NY 10016 USA

Great Clarendon Street, Oxford OX2 6DP UK

Oxford University Press is a department of the University of Oxford.
It furthers the University's objective of excellence in research,
scholarship, and education by publishing worldwide in

Oxford New York
Auckland Cape Town Dar es Salaam Hong Kong Karachi
Kuala Lumpur Madrid Melbourne Mexico City Nairobi
New Delhi Shanghai Taipei Toronto

With offices in
Argentina Austria Brazil Chile Czech Republic France Greece
Guatemala Hungary Italy Japan Poland Portugal Singapore
South Korea Switzerland Thailand Turkey Ukraine Vietnam

OXFORD and OXFORD ENGLISH are registered trademarks of
Oxford University Press.

Editorial Director: Laura Pearson
Executive Publishing Manager: Stephanie Karras
Managing Editor: Sharon Sargent
Associate Development Editor: Olga Christopoulos
Design Director: Susan Sanguily
Design Manager: Maj-Britt Hagsted
Design Assistant: Karen Vanderbilt
Project Coordinator: Sarah Dentry
Cover Design: Stacy Merlin
Senior Image Editor: Justine Eun
Manufacturing Manager: Shanta Persaud
Manufacturing Coordinator: Faye Wang

ISBN: 978 0 19 430196 1 OPD Assessment Program (pack)
ISBN: 978 0 19 430197 8 OPD Assessment Program (book)
ISBN: 978 0 19 430198 5 Assessment CD-ROM

Printed in Hong Kong

10 9 8 7 6 5 4 3 2 1

Illustrations by: David Cain: 3, 5, 47, 48, 87; Tom Newsom: 11, 18, 19, 20,
27, 29, 30, 41, 61, 76, 78, 80, 88, 90, 98; Karen Pietrobono: 29, 77, 79, 87,
88; Zina Saunders: 32, 34, 57, 61, 62, 71, 72, 73, 74, 75; Tom Sperling: 5,
11, 15, 20, 22, 32, 33, 34, 37, 38, 39, 40, 41, 42, 43, 44, 46, 54, 83, 86;
Gary Undercuffler: 7, 21, 33, 49, 53, 54, 56, 79, 105, 106; Patrick J. Welsh:
17, 42, 58, 59, 60, 77.

Chapter icons designed by Von Glitschka/Scott Hull Associates.

Cover art by CUBE/Illustration Ltd. (hummingbird); 9 Surf Studios
(lettering).

Table of Contents

Contents

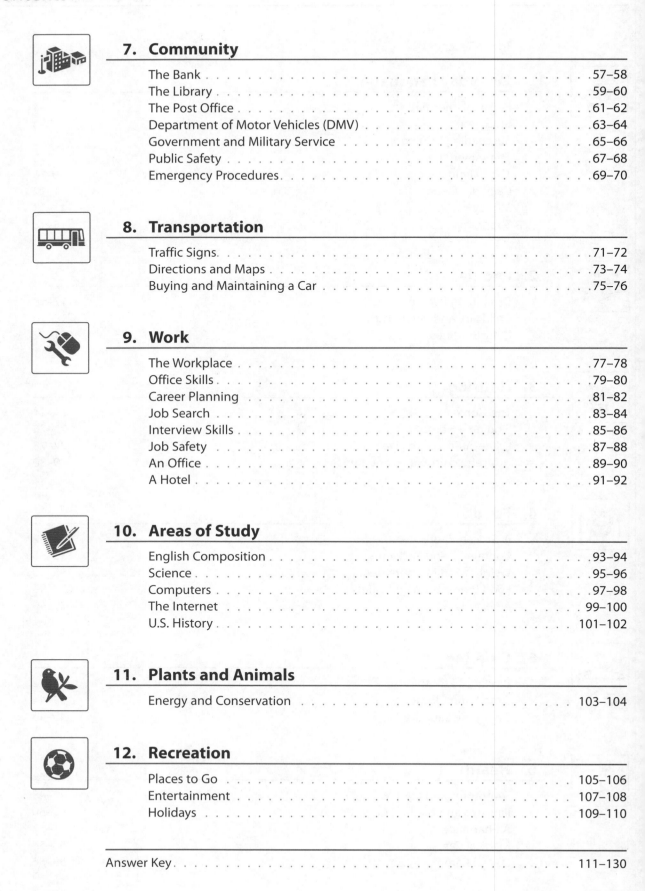

What is the *Oxford Picture Dictionary Second Edition Assessment Program*?

With the *Oxford Picture Dictionary Second Edition Assessment Program,* you can create customized tests for use with the second edition of the *Oxford Picture Dictionary*. These tests will help you assess student progress at any phase of the learning process. You can use the reproducible tests in the book or create tests using the testing software as placement tests, pre-tests, topic-by-topic tests, unit-by-unit tests, mid-terms, or final exams, depending on your specific class needs. The *Assessment Program* will help students to gauge their own progress based on test results. In addition, the *OPD 2e Assessment CD-ROM's* Life-Skill Reading tests provide you with the ability to test by students' ability levels: low beginning, high beginning, and low intermediate.

What is included in the *Assessment Program* book?

The book includes 55 tests in an easy-to-use reproducible format. These tests are selected from the complete bank of Topic Tests featured on the *Assessment CD-ROM* and test 10 to 15 high-frequency words from each *OPD* topic. The 55 reproducible tests cover the topics linked to the most common life-skill, civics, and workplace objectives.

What is included on the *Assessment CD-ROM*?

The *Assessment CD-ROM*, found on the inside back cover of this book, is test-generating software for creating customized tests. It includes over 4,000 test items in familiar question formats: true/false, multiple choice, and fill-in-the-blank.

There are two kinds of question banks on the *Assessment CD-ROM*:

- ▸ The OPD Topic Question Bank, with a test item for every vocabulary term in the *OPD*.

- ▸ The OPD Reading Question Bank, which contains 12 Low Beginning Reading Tests, 16 High Beginning Reading Tests, and 12 Low Intermediate Reading Tests. Each test consists of 10 items.

The *Assessment CD-ROM* provides a Topic Test for each of the 166 topics in the *OPD*. Choose items from the OPD Topic Question Bank to determine the vocabulary terms that students already know, their areas of weakness, and to help you prepare tests that are customized to the vocabulary terms students need or want to learn. Please see below for how you can **select specific questions** from a bank.

Because adult ESL classes commonly include students working at various levels, the *OPD* series addresses the needs of students and teachers working in a multilevel environment. The leveled Reading Question Bank evaluates learners' life-skill reading comprehension and allows all students to be tested on the **same** *OPD* unit, but in a manner appropriate to their individual levels.

How can I create tests using the *Assessment CD-ROM*?

You can easily create tests in a number of ways.

- ▸ **Print out a Topic Test directly from the CD-ROM without any changes:** One hundred sixty-six Topic Tests, one for every topic in the *OPD*, are provided in the **OPD Topic Question Bank**. Simply click an *OPD* topic, select the items you would like to include in your test (selecting all items will allow you to test every vocabulary term in the topic), then click *File* and *Print*.

- ▸ **Print out a Reading Test directly from the CD-ROM without any changes:** Reading Tests for each unit in the *OPD* are provided in the **OPD Reading Question Bank**. Click the test you would like to print, choosing by *OPD* unit and level, select the items you would like to test, then click *File* and *Print*.

- ▸ **Create a customized test in just minutes:** Use the *Filter by* function to select the type and number of questions you want to include from each question bank. You can choose by:
  - question type
  - difficulty
  - objective
  - vocabulary term
  - reference (*OPD* topic)
  - standard (CASAS Life Skill Competencies)

- ▸ **Write your own questions:** Create completely new tests using items you've written, or edit the questions provided. Use the *Show Me How To…* feature for guidance through each step involved in creating tests.

To the Teacher

All tests can be printed out for students. Test questions can be scrambled to appear in any order, and you can save all your tests on a computer to use for future classes. An answer key is automatically generated for each test you create. To change the appearance of your printed tests (e.g. to include the test name at the top of the page), click *File* and *Page Setup*.

For easy, step-by-step instructions for using the test-generating software on the *Assessment CD-ROM,* see the **Quick-Start Manual** PDF on the CD-ROM. From *My Computer* on your desktop, right-click on the OPD CD icon and select *Open*.

How will the *Assessment Program* help students on standardized tests?

The entire *Assessment Program* is standards-based. Every test item is correlated to the Comprehensive Adult Student Assessment System (CASAS).

Because students also need experience and practice taking standardized tests, the majority of *OPD Assessment Program* test items are multiple choice. In addition, there are at least three leveled Life-Skill Reading tests for each unit in the *OPD*.

How does the *Assessment Program* work with the *Oxford Picture Dictionary* program?

As with all *OPD 2e* components, the *Assessment Program* is part of a complete vocabulary development program. However you choose to use the *Assessment Program*—by using the photocopiable exams in the book, printing out the complete Topic and Reading Tests on the CD-ROM, or creating your own tests—it can help you diagnose students' instructional needs, monitor progress, and certify mastery of all *OPD* vocabulary.

Personal Information

Name _____ Date _____

Choose the best answer.

_____ 1. My _____ is (212) 555-7865 .
   a. address
   b. phone number
   c. Social Security number
   d. date of birth

_____ 2. The address is _____.
   a. 25 East Mellon Street
   b. July 22nd, 1950
   c. (213) 555-7865
   d. 6/18/07

_____ 3. _____ *your name* means to write your signature.
   a. *Say*
   b. *Sign*
   c. *Print*
   d. *Spell*

_____ 4. My _____ is Mike S. Wallace.
   a. apartment number
   b. name
   c. address
   d. street

Look at Jose's information. Choose the best answer.

Jose T. Vargas
127 Harold Street #3
Brooklyn, NY 11205

_____ 5. *Brooklyn* is the _____.
   a. city
   b. state
   c. sex
   d. apartment number

_____ **6.** *NY* is the _____ .

    a. last name

    b. state

    c. date of birth

    d. middle initial

Complete the dialogue.

_____ **7. A:** What's your _____ ?

    B: It's 10018.

    a. phone number

    b. Social Security number

    c. ZIP code

    d. date of birth

_____ **8. A:** Please _____ your name.

    B: A-n-d-y.

    a. print

    b. say

    c. spell

    d. sign

_____ **9. A:** Is _____ your date of birth?

    B: Yes, it is.

    a. 3/28/65

    b. London

    c. Staten Island

    d. (212) 555-2956

Complete the sentence.

10. Wendy's _____ is *female*.

Name _____ Date _____

Write T (true) or F (false).

_____ **1.** You put away your books in your backpack.

Choose the best answer.

_____ **2.** There are two students and one book. They can _____ the book.
  a. draw
  b. share
  c. circle
  d. cross out

_____ **3.** This is _____.
  a. *draw a picture*
  b. *copy a word*
  c. *discuss a problem*
  d. *dictate a sentence*

_____ **4.** This is _____ *the correct answer* .
  a. *put*
  b. *choose*
  c. *dictate*
  d. *share*

Which do you read?
a. book
b. desk
c. chair

_____ **5.** Please open your notebooks and _____ the words on the board.
  a. ask
  b. help
  c. copy
  d. draw

_____ **6.** _____ a piece of paper and copy the words on the board.
  a. Put away
  b. Take out
  c. Cross out
  d. Fill in

Complete the dialogue.

_____ 7. **A:** Please _____ .

       B: OK. What's your ZIP code?

       a. ask a question

       b. answer a question

       c. discuss a problem

       d. copy a word

Look at the dialogue. Choose the best answer.

    Mike: There's no bulletin board in the classroom!

    John: Yeah, and there's no clock!

    Paul: Talk to the teacher.

    Sonya: Talk to the principal, too.

_____ 8. Mike and John _____ .

       a. brainstorm solutions

       b. help a classmate

       c. discuss problems

       d. dictate a sentence

_____ 9. Paul and Sonya _____ .

       a. brainstorm solutions

       b. help a classmate

       c. discuss problems

       d. dictate a sentence

_____ 10. Mike, John, Paul, and Sonya _____ .

       a. share a book

       b. read the definition

       c. translate words

       d. work in a group

Succeeding in School

Name _____ Date _____

Write T (true) or F (false).

_____ 1. A grade of F means you passed the test.

_____ 2. This is *study at home*.

Choose the best answer.

_____ 3. This is _____.
- **a.** *ask for help*
- **b.** *bubble in the answer*
- **c.** *clear off your desk*
- **d.** *take notes*

_____ 4. You are taking a test. You should _____.
- **a.** set goals
- **b.** participate in class
- **c.** study at home
- **d.** check your work

_____ 5. Wow! 99/100! That's a great _____.
- **a.** test booklet
- **b.** score
- **c.** answer sheet
- **d.** test

_____ 6. Please bubble in the answers on the _____.
- **a.** score
- **b.** answer sheet
- **c.** goals
- **d.** grades

_____ 7. My name is spelled *David*, NOT *Daved*. Please _____.
   a. correct the mistake
   b. clear off your desk
   c. pass a test
   d. set goals

_____ 8. Please take a seat and open your _____.
   a. answer sheet
   b. scores
   c. grades
   d. test booklet

Complete the dialogue.

_____ 9. **A:** I don't understand.

   B: Ask for _____.
   a. goals
   b. progress
   c. help
   d. class

_____ 10. **A:** I am finished checking my work.

   B: Good. Now _____ your test.
   a. hand in
   b. bubble in
   c. clear off
   d. study

The Telephone

Name _____ Date _____

Write T (true) or F (false).

_____ **1.** You dial a phone number on the key pad.

_____ **2.** A calling card is for a smart phone.

_____ **3.** The pound key is #.

_____ **4.** The star key is $.

_____ **5.** Dial 911 to make an emergency phone call.

_____ **6.** A cellular phone has a charger.

_____ **7.** This is an answering machine.

Choose the best answer.

_____ **8.** _____ "send" to make a phone call.
    a. Give
    b. State
    c. Stay
    d. Press

_____ **9.** _____ the phone number.
    a. Dial
    b. Talk
    c. Hang up
    d. Stay

_____ **10.** A phone call from New York to Paris is _____.
    a. a smart phone
    b. an international call
    c. a local call
    d. a long distance call

_____ **11.** A phone call from New York to Chicago is _____.
   a. a text message
   b. an international call
   c. a local call
   d. a long distance call

_____ **12.** A phone call from 15 Smith Street to 16 Smith Street is _____.
   a. a local call
   b. an international call
   c. a pound key
   d. a long distance call

_____ **13.** You write a _____.
   a. text message
   b. TDD
   c. voice message
   d. headset

_____ **14.** A _____ is NOT part of a phone.
   a. cord
   b. key pad
   c. receiver
   d. voice message

_____ **15.** Pick up the _____.
   a. country code
   b. operator
   c. receiver
   d. pound key

The Calendar

Name _____   Date _____

Write T (true) or F (false).

_____ **1.** Monday is on the weekend.

_____ **2.** December 12th, 2008, is a date.

_____ **3.** July is a season.

_____ **4.** May is a date.

Choose the best answer.

_____ **5.** Today is Tuesday. _____ is Wednesday.
   a. Tomorrow
   b. Yesterday
   c. Next week
   d. This week

_____ **6.** _____ is NOT a month.
   a. January
   b. August
   c. Thursday
   d. October

_____ **7.** Today is Sunday. Saturday was _____.
   a. autumn
   b. Thursday
   c. next week
   d. yesterday

_____ **8.** June is the sixth _____ of the year.
   a. day
   b. month
   c. season
   d. weekend

_____ 9. Tuesday and Saturday are _____.
   a. months
   b. weeks
   c. years
   d. days

_____ 10. _____ is Tuesday. Tomorrow is Wednesday.
   a. Every day
   b. Today
   c. Twice a week
   d. Yesterday

_____ 11. _____ is the first month of the year.
   a. September
   b. January
   c. Tuesday
   d. Spring

_____ 12. There are 31 days in _____.
   a. winter
   b. summer
   c. March
   d. fall

Complete the dialogue.

_____ 13. A: What's your date of birth?
       B: _____ 18th, 1968.
          a. October
          b. Fall
          c. Winter
          d. Tuesday

Complete the sentence.

14. A _____ has 12 months.

15. The weekend is Saturday and _____.

Name _____ Date _____

Write T (true) or F (false).

_____ 1.  This is a wedding.

_____ 2.  This book is for appointments.

_____ 3. New Year's Day is February 1st.

_____ 4. Veterans Day is in March.

_____ 5. People have two birthdays every year.

_____ 6. We don't eat on Thanksgiving.

_____ 7. Presidents' Day is a calendar event.

Choose the best answer.

_____ 8. _____ is a legal holiday.
- **a.** A parent-teacher conference
- **b.** A wedding
- **c.** A birthday
- **d.** Memorial Day

_____ 9. Martin Luther King Jr. Day is in _____.
- **a.** December
- **b.** July
- **c.** January
- **d.** September

_____ **10.** Which is NOT a legal holiday?

    a. Presidents' Day

    b. Thanksgiving

    c. a religious holiday

    d. Veterans Day

_____ **11.** Which holiday is in September?

    a. Labor Day

    b. Memorial Day

    c. New Year's Day

    d. Columbus Day

Complete the sentence.

12. _____ is December 25th.

13. Memorial Day and Veterans' Day are _____ holidays.

14. Columbus Day is in the month of _____.

15. We watch fireworks on the _____.

Money

Name _____ Date _____

Write T (true) or F (false).

_____ **1.** $.10 = a dime.

_____ **2.** $100.00 = ten dollars.

_____ **3.** $.50 = five dollars.

Choose the best answer.

_____ **4.** $.01 = _____.
- **a.** a penny
- **b.** 25 cents
- **c.** 5 cents
- **d.** a half dollar

_____ **5.** Four _____ = one dollar.
- **a.** dimes
- **b.** quarters
- **c.** pennies
- **d.** nickels

_____ **6.** There are ten dimes in _____.
- **a.** a dollar
- **b.** five dollars
- **c.** twenty dollars
- **d.** thirty dollars

_____ **7.** $100.00 = _____.
- **a.** fifty dollars
- **b.** one dollar
- **c.** ten dollars
- **d.** one hundred dollars

Complete the dialogue.

_____ **8. A:** Can I _____ some money?

      B: Sure. Please pay me back next week.

        a. get

        b. lend

        c. borrow

        d. pay back

_____ **9. A:** Can I borrow a dollar?

      B: Sorry, I don't like to _____ money.

        a. get

        b. borrow

        c. lend

        d. pay back

Complete the sentence.

10. A _____ is 5 cents.

Shopping

Name _____ Date _____

Write T (true) or F (false).

_____ **1.** *Buy* and *pay for* are the same.

_____ **2.** You are returning something. You give the cashier money.

_____ **3.** You use a gift card in the classroom.

_____ **4.** He's using a credit card to buy the items.

Choose the best answer.

_____ **5.** Please pay _____.
    a. cash
    b. the SKU number
    c. the bar code
    d. the gift card

_____ **6.** I can write _____.
    a. cash
    b. a credit card
    c. a check
    d. a gift card

_____ **7.** The total is on your _____.
    a. bar code
    b. price tag
    c. receipt
    d. cash

Complete the dialogue.

_____ **8.** **A:** I don't like this pen.

B: You can _____ it.
- **a.** buy
- **b.** cash
- **c.** pay for
- **d.** exchange

_____ **9.** **A:** I have no cash.

B: Use _____ .
- **a.** a debit card
- **b.** a cash register
- **c.** a price tag
- **d.** an SKU number

_____ **10.** **A:** What is the _____ of that lamp?

B: The price tag says $15.95.
- **a.** SKU number
- **b.** cash register
- **c.** bar code
- **d.** cost

Describing People

Name _____   Date _____

Write T (true) or F (false).

_____ **1.** Sara is a 1-year-old girl. She is elderly.

_____ **2.** Ali is 7 feet tall. He is short.

Choose the best answer.

_____ **3.** Babies are _____.
    a. cute
    b. pregnant
    c. elderly
    d. middle-aged

_____ **4.** Juanita is 22 years old. She is _____.
    a. middle-aged
    b. elderly
    c. average height
    d. young

_____ **5.** Brad runs every day. He is _____.
    a. thin
    b. heavy
    c. blind
    d. elderly

_____ **6.** John weighs 200 pounds and is 5 feet tall. He is _____.
    a. thin
    b. heavy
    c. sight impaired
    d. pregnant

_____ **7.** Lilian is 45 years old. She is _____.
    a. elderly
    b. middle-aged
    c. young
    d. slender

_____ **8.** Mena is going to have a baby. She is _____.

    a. elderly

    b. tall

    c. short

    d. pregnant

Complete the dialogue.

_____ **9.** **A:** Can you help me? I can't reach the high shelf.

    B: Yes, I can help you. I am _____.

    a. short

    b. tall

    c. thin

    d. slender

_____ **10.** **A:** Is Monica a model?

    B: Yes, she is very _____.

    a. attractive

    b. heavy

    c. pregnant

    d. elderly

Name _____   Date _____

Write T (true) or F (false).

_____ **1.** Diapers, bottles, and wipes go in the baby bag.

_____ **2.** I kiss the baby goodnight when she wakes up.

Choose the best answer.

_____ **3.** I _____ a lullaby to make the baby fall asleep.
  a. praise
  b. sing
  c. rock
  d. read

_____ **4.** Mommy pushes my little brother in a _____ every day.
  a. baby carrier
  b. rocking chair
  c. stroller
  d. car safety seat

_____ **5.** Little Lucia wants to eat. Can you _____ her?
  a. dress
  b. rock
  c. change
  d. feed

_____ **6.** Charlie loves books. I _____ him every day.
  a. read to
  b. nurse
  c. play with
  d. dress

Complete the dialogue.

_____ **7. A:** The baby is crying again.

B: Oh, I see the problem. It's time to
_____ his diaper.
    a. change
    b. hold
    c. rock
    d. feed

_____ **8. A:** Mommy, I have a new toy!

B: Great! Let's _____ it.
    a. feed
    b. play with
    c. nurse
    d. rock

_____ **9. A:** I think he's asleep.

B: Can I _____ him for a while?
    a. hold
    b. change
    c. feed
    d. dress

Complete the sentence.

10. We need to _____ the baby in warm water.

Name _____   Date _____

Write T (true) or F (false).

_____ **1.** Most people have dinner at 8:00 a.m.

_____ **2.** Many people cook dinner at 6:00 p.m.

Choose the best answer.

_____ **3.** Which do you do first?
- **a.** get up
- **b.** get dressed
- **c.** eat breakfast
- **d.** take a shower

_____ **4.** Which one means *get into bed*?
- **a.** wake up
- **b.** get dressed
- **c.** go to bed
- **d.** get up

_____ **5.** Lili _____ from 9:00 a.m. to 5:00 p.m.
- **a.** eats breakfast
- **b.** works
- **c.** leaves work
- **d.** wakes up

_____ **6.** I _____ every morning.
- **a.** get up
- **b.** wake up
- **c.** get dressed
- **d.** take a shower

_____ **7.** Let's ride bikes to the park. I need to _____ .
- **a.** go to sleep
- **b.** exercise
- **c.** eat breakfast
- **d.** watch TV

Look at Jin's schedule. Choose the best answer.

Jin Young's schedule

Monday	
7:00 a.m.	get up
8:00 a.m. – 12:00 p.m.	go to school
12:30 p.m.	make lunch
2:00 p.m.	go to work

_____ **8.** What does Jin Young do at 12:30 p.m.?

    a. get up

    b. go to school

    c. make lunch

    d. go to work

Complete the dialogue.

_____ **9.** **A:** How does the woman go to work?

    B: She _____ to work.

    a. drives

    b. takes the bus

    c. runs

    d. walks

_____ **10.** **A:** What does Sandy do when the house is dirty?

    B: She _____ .

    a. cleans the house

    b. does homework

    c. watches TV

    d. exercises

The Home

Name _____ Date _____

Write T (true) or F (false).

_____ **1.** You can open and close a door.

_____ **2.** The basement is at the top of the house.

_____ **3.** We eat food in the bathroom.

Choose the best answer.

_____ **4.** We sleep in the _____.
    a. kitchen
    b. bathroom
    c. bedroom
    d. dining area

_____ **5.** John cooks dinner in the _____.
    a. baby's room
    b. living room
    c. bedroom
    d. kitchen

_____ **6.** Which is easy to break?
    a. a window
    b. a dining area
    c. a bedroom
    d. an attic

_____ **7.** The sofa is in the _____.
    a. door
    b. living room
    c. bathroom
    d. kitchen

_____ **8.** Please put the chair on the _____ in the living room.

     a. door

     b. roof

     c. window

     d. floor

_____ **9.** We eat lunch next to the kitchen in the _____.

     a. baby's room

     b. kids' room

     c. dining area

     d. garage

_____ **10.** A _____ is a place for your car.

     a. floor

     b. roof

     c. basement

     d. garage

Finding a Home

Name _____ Date _____

Write T (true) or F (false).

_____ **1.** You can get a loan at a bank.

_____ **2.** You take ownership of a house when you sell it.

Choose the best answer.

_____ **3.** You _____ when you move into a new home.
- **a.** unpack
- **b.** look at houses
- **c.** call the manager
- **d.** pack

_____ **4.** I own my house. It is important to _____ every month.
- **a.** sign a rental agreement
- **b.** make a mortgage payment
- **c.** get a loan
- **d.** pay the first and last month's rent

Complete the dialogue.

_____ **5. A:** We are having a baby. We want to buy a house.

B: You can _____ .
- **a.** pay the utilities
- **b.** meet with a realtor
- **c.** unpack
- **d.** sign the rental agreement

_____ **6. A:** How much is the rent?

B: I don't know. _____
- **a.** Arrange the furniture.
- **b.** Get a loan.
- **c.** Move in.
- **d.** Call the manager.

_____ 7. **A:** I don't like where I live.

    B: Do you want to _____?

       a. pay the first and last month's rent

       b. look at houses

       c. sign the rental agreement

       d. pack

_____ 8. **A:** I am looking for a new apartment on the computer.

    B: So, you are looking at _____.

       a. a furnished apartment

       b. an unfurnished apartment

       c. Internet listings

       d. a utility

_____ 9. **A:** We should have our first party in the new house.

    B: Great! We can _____.

       a. meet the neighbors

       b. unpack

       c. pack

       d. pay the first and last month's rent

Complete the sentence.

10. A place to rent with furniture in it is a _____.

11. Electricity, gas, and cable are _____.

12. The newspaper has _____ for houses and apartments.

13. We are moving next week. Please _____ the boxes.

14. I want to _____ the house yellow on Saturday.

15. I am renting an apartment. I have to sign a _____ before I can move in.

Different Places to Live

Name _____ Date _____

Write T (true) or F (false).

_____ **1.** There are many tall buildings, offices, and cars in the suburbs.

_____ **2.** This is a townhouse.

_____ **3.** The country is a quiet, rural area.

Choose the best answer.

_____ **4.** Many college students live in a _____.
    a. shelter
    b. nursing home
    c. mobile home
    d. college dormitory

_____ **5.** Children do NOT live here.
    a. a mobile home
    b. a townhouse
    c. a nursing home
    d. a farm

_____ **6.** Hector lives _____. He grows corn, wheat, and potatoes.
    a. in a shelter
    b. on a farm
    c. in a nursing home
    d. in a condominium

Complete the dialogue.

_____ 7. **A:** Is it quiet where you live?

      B: No. I live in _____ . It's very noisy.
- **a.** the city
- **b.** the suburbs
- **c.** the country
- **d.** a small town

_____ 8. **A:** I am moving to a small town. I am bringing my home with me.

      B: Oh, you have a _____ .
- **a.** townhouse
- **b.** nursing home
- **c.** college dormitory
- **d.** mobile home

_____ 9. **A:** I live in Douglaston. About 10,000 people live there.

      B: Douglaston is a _____ .
- **a.** ranch
- **b.** small town
- **c.** shelter
- **d.** nursing home

_____ 10. **A:** I want to live in the city, but it is too expensive.

      B: You can buy a _____ . It is not as expensive as a house.
- **a.** condominium
- **b.** college dormitory
- **c.** ranch
- **d.** shelter

Household Problems and Repairs

Name _____   Date _____

Write T (true) or F (false).

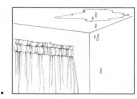

_____ **1.**   The roof is leaking.

_____ **2.**   This woman is a locksmith.

Choose the best answer.

_____ **3.**   A _____ uses this tool to fix water pipes.

a. plumber
b. locksmith
c. roofer
d. carpenter

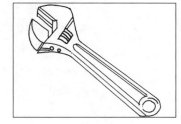

_____ **4.**   There are termites in Jordan's house. He calls _____.

a. a roofer
b. a repair person
c. a plumber
d. an exterminator

_____ **5.**   Which household pests eat wood?

a. fleas
b. termites
c. cockroaches
d. rats

Complete the dialogue.

_____ **6. A:** Turn on the TV.

B: Sorry, I can't. The power is _____ .
   a. dripping
   b. out
   c. cracked
   d. stopped up

_____ **7. A:** Why is there water on the bathroom floor?

B: _____
   a. The lock is broken.
   b. The power is out.
   c. The furnace is broken.
   d. The sink is overflowing.

_____ **8. A:** I can't turn on the lights!

B: You need to call _____ .
   a. an electrician
   b. a roofer
   c. a carpenter
   d. a plumber

Complete the sentence.

9. This window is _____ . Can you fix it?

10. The roof is leaking. The _____ is fixing it.

A Grocery Store

Name _____   Date _____

Write T (true) or F (false).

_____ 1. You pay a cashier for your food.

_____ 2. You can put your food in a cart.

_____ 3. The manager of a market puts food in bags.

_____ 4. A bagger sells paper bags.

_____ 5. You stand in line after you pay for your food.

_____ 6. You walk in the aisle in a grocery store.

Choose the best answer.

_____ 7. Tuna is usually in the _____ section.
   a. Beverages
   b. Baking Products
   c. Dairy
   d. Canned Foods

_____ 8. You can find _____ in the Dairy section.
   a. cookies
   b. beans
   c. yogurt
   d. apple juice

_____ 9. You can cook chicken in _____.
   a. sugar
   b. oil
   c. coffee
   d. soda

_____ 10. You do NOT find _____ in the Dairy section.
   a. sugar
   b. margarine
   c. yogurt
   d. sour cream

_____ **11.** You can find _____ in the Canned Foods section.

    a. frozen vegetables

    b. beans

    c. cake

    d. cookies

Complete the dialogue.

_____ **12.** **A:** What else do we need to make this cake?

    B: We need to add some _____ .

    a. tuna

    b. frozen vegetables

    c. potato chips

    d. flour

_____ **13.** **A:** Do you want to eat something cold and sweet?

    B: Yes. I want a bowl of _____ .

    a. cookies

    b. ice cream

    c. cake

    d. candy bars

Complete the sentence.

14. Please don't buy any _____ . I don't like sweet things.

15. A person shopping in a grocery store is a _____ .

Name _____   Date _____

Write T (true) or F (false).

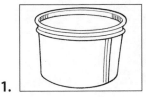

_____ 1. This picture shows a container.

_____ 2. Cans are made of plastic.

Choose the best answer.

_____ 3. Six cans make a _____.
     a. package
     b. carton
     c. container
     d. six-pack

_____ 4. Many people buy rice in a _____.
     a. can
     b. carton
     c. box
     d. bottle

_____ 5. You can see what is inside a _____.
     a. jar
     b. tube
     c. can
     d. carton

_____ 6. This is a _____ of toothpaste.
     a. roll
     b. tube
     c. can
     d. bag

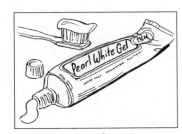

_____ **7.** Can you buy a _____ of bread?

    a. loaf

    b. box

    c. carton

    d. container

_____ **8.** Potato chips come in _____ .

    a. jars

    b. loaves

    c. bags

    d. cartons

Complete the sentence.

9. You can buy ketchup in a _____ .

10. Robert, can you make breakfast?

We have a _____ .

Weights and Measurements

Name _____ Date _____

Write T (true) or F (false).

_____ 1. You weigh food to find out how heavy it is.

_____ 2. You measure the ingredients that go in a cake.

Choose the best answer.

_____ 3. Please buy a _____ of water at the market.
   a. teaspoon
   b. tablespoon
   c. half cup
   d. gallon

_____ 4. Add _____ of cheese to the pasta salad.
   a. an ounce
   b. a fluid ounce
   c. a pint
   d. a quart

_____ 5. Please buy _____ of frozen yogurt at the store.
   a. a fluid ounce
   b. a pint
   c. an ounce
   d. a pound

_____ 6. I'm going to add a _____ of sugar to this glass of iced tea.
   a. pound
   b. gallon
   c. tablespoon
   d. cup

_____ 7. A _____ of oil is the biggest.
   a. teaspoon
   b. cup
   c. tablespoon
   d. half cup

Complete the dialogue.

_____ 8. **A:** What do you have to add to the cookies?

B: I need _____ of salt.

    a. a teaspoon

    b. a fluid ounce

    c. a cup

    d. a gallon

_____ 9. **A:** What are you buying to make sandwiches?

B: I'm buying _____ of roast beef.

    a. a gallon

    b. a pound

    c. a cup

    d. a fluid ounce

_____ 10. **A:** These cookies are not too sweet.

B: No, they have only _____ .

    a. a teaspoon of salt

    b. a quart of milk

    c. a quarter cup of brown sugar

    d. a cup of brown sugar

Food Preparation and Safety

Name _____ Date _____

Write T (true) or F (false).

_____ **1.** Scrambled eggs are cooked in the oven.

_____ **2.** You can boil ham.

Choose the best answer.

_____ **3.** _____ turkey is cooked in the oven.
    a. Fried
    b. Roasted
    c. Boiled
    d. Stir-fried

_____ **4.** Which kind of meat is cooked in oil?
    a. roasted turkey
    b. boiled ham
    c. broiled steak
    d. fried chicken

_____ **5.** I am making chicken soup. I am going to _____ the chicken.
    a. boil
    b. grate
    c. bake
    d. chill

_____ **6.** _____ the cake at 350°.
    a. Fry
    b. Bake
    c. Boil
    d. Simmer

Complete the dialogue.

_____ 7. **A:** Can I help make dinner?

B: OK. Please _____ the broccoli.
  a. steam
  b. break
  c. beat
  d. grate

_____ 8. **A:** Do you want ribs tonight?

B: Sure, let's _____ some.
  a. grate
  b. mix
  c. barbecue
  d. peel

_____ 9. **A:** How do I make chicken soup?

B: First, _____ .
  a. simmer
  b. boil the chicken
  c. cut up the chicken
  d. stir

Complete the sentence.

10. Please _____ the carrots.

Name _____ Date _____

Write T (true) or F (false).

_____ 1. A busser drives people to a restaurant.

_____ 2. A menu shows all the food you can order in a restaurant.

Choose the best answer.

_____ 3. The woman is _____.
   a. bussing the dishes
   b. setting the table
   c. pouring the water
   d. serving the meal

_____ 4. I am very full! Now let's _____ and leave.
   a. set the table
   b. pay the check
   c. serve the meal
   d. pour the water

_____ 5. The patron _____ for the server.
   a. clears the dishes
   b. carries the tray
   c. leaves a tip
   d. sets the table

Complete the dialogue.

_____ 6. **A:** I know what I want to eat.

   B: Here is the waitress. She can _____.
   a. pay the check
   b. take the order
   c. clear the dishes
   d. leave a tip

_____ 7. **A:** My daughter is too small to eat at the table.

    B: Do you want a _____ for her?

    a. high chair

    b. dessert tray

    c. place setting

    d. menu

_____ 8. **A:** Is the man eating?

    B: No, he is _____ .

    a. leaving a tip

    b. taking the order

    c. ordering from the menu

    d. pouring the water

_____ 9. **A:** Let's get some more rolls.

    B: Ask the _____ for some.

    a. waiter

    b. hostess

    c. dishwasher

    d. chef

Complete the sentence.

10. This server is a woman. She is a _____ .

Name _____ Date _____

Write T (true) or F (false).

_____ **1.** This is a work shirt.

_____ **2.** A construction worker wears a lab coat.

_____ **3.** You wear an apron on your feet.

Choose the best answer.

_____ **4.** A medical technician wears a _____ over his mouth.
   a. badge
   b. face mask
   c. helmet
   d. bump cap

_____ **5.** A _____ is used to protect your head.
   a. hard hat
   b. cowboy hat
   c. bandana
   d. hairnet

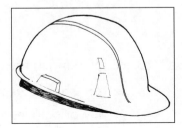

_____ **6.** A nurse wears _____ in the hospital.
   a. coveralls
   b. scrubs
   c. a blazer
   d. a chef's jacket

Complete the dialogue.

_____ **7. A:** What do you wear to work?

B: I wear a _____ every day.
   a. blazer
   b. security shirt
   c. work shirt
   d. polo shirt

_____ **8. A:** What is that on your shirt?

B: It's my _____ . It tells people who I am.
   a. apron
   b. name tag
   c. tool belt
   d. smock

_____ **9. A:** Excuse me. Do you work here?

B: Yes. I am the security guard. Here is
   my _____ .
   a. blazer
   b. tie
   c. hairnet
   d. badge

_____ **10. A:** Working in the garden hurts my hands.

B: You should wear your _____ .
   a. work gloves
   b. surgical mask
   c. bump cap
   d. badge

Describing Clothes

Name _____ Date _____

Write T (true) or F (false).

_____ 1. This is a short-sleeved shirt.

Choose the best answer.

_____ 2. This is a _____ tie.
  a. polka-dotted
  b. narrow
  c. wide
  d. checked

_____ 3. A _____ covers your knees.
  a. loose skirt
  b. short skirt
  c. mini-skirt
  d. long skirt

_____ 4. Which is a size?
  a. large
  b. plaid
  c. print
  d. striped

_____ 5. These shoes are _____ . Let's find a bigger size.
  a. stained
  b. too small
  c. extra large
  d. too expensive

_____ **6.** A _____ jacket is good for cool weather.

    a. light

    b. plaid

    c. striped

    d. fancy

Complete the dialogue.

_____ **7.** **A:** What size is that sweater?

    B: It's _____ .

    a. fancy

    b. light

    c. medium

    d. plaid

_____ **8.** **A:** Are you going to buy that skirt?

    B: No. It's _____ . I want a long skirt.

    a. floral

    b. short

    c. wide

    d. polka-dotted

Complete the sentence.

9. I want to buy this suit with

a _____ pattern.

10. This tie isn't narrow. It's a _____ .

Doing the Laundry

Name _____ Date _____

Choose the best answer.

_____ **1.** Which cleans clothes?
    a. spray starch
    b. laundry detergent
    c. dryer sheets
    d. fabric softener

_____ **2.** Please hang the _____ on the clothesline to dry.
    a. ironed shirt
    b. dryer sheets
    c. lint trap
    d. laundry

_____ **3.** I need to do something to this shirt. It's wrinkled! Where is the _____ ?
    a. clothesline
    b. lint trap
    c. ironing board
    d. fabric softener

_____ **4.** _____ means to put the clothes on hangers.
    a. *Fold the laundry*
    b. *Hang up the clothes*
    c. *Iron the clothes*
    d. *Clean the lint trap*

_____ **5.** _____ is a machine that cleans clothes.
    a. A laundry basket
    b. A washer
    c. A dryer
    d. An iron

_____ **6.** Be careful! The _____ is hot.
    a. bleach
    b. iron
    c. clothespin
    d. hanger

_____ 7. Please take the wet clothes out of the washer. Put them in the _____ for 30 minutes.

    a. laundry basket

    b. ironing board

    c. lint trap

    d. dryer

Complete the dialogue.

_____ 8. **A:** These clothes are wrinkled. Do we have any spray starch?

    B: No, but you can _____ without it.

    a. dry the clothes

    b. iron the clothes

    c. fold the clothes

    d. clean the clothes

_____ 9. **A:** The clothes are out of the dryer now.

    B: Can I help you _____?

    a. add the detergent

    b. unload the dryer

    c. fold the laundry

    d. load the washer

Complete the sentence.

10. This ironed shirt is on a _____.

Symptoms and Injuries

Name _____ Date _____

Write T (true) or F (false).

_____ 1. A toothache means that your tooth hurts.

_____ 2. An earache means that your eyes hurt.

Choose the best answer.

_____ 3. Which of these can make it hard to stand up straight?
   a. rash
   b. cut
   c. toothache
   d. backache

_____ 4. Which is NOT a skin injury?
   a. sunburn
   b. blister
   c. headache
   d. cut

_____ 5. It's a good idea to sit down when you _____.
   a. cough
   b. sneeze
   c. have a sunburn
   d. feel dizzy

_____ 6. Ouch! I have a _____ on my finger.
   a. sunburn
   b. bruise
   c. cut
   d. rash

Complete the dialogue.

_____ 7. **A:** How are you?

    B: I can't talk. I have a _____ .

       a. rash

       b. backache

       c. sore throat

       d. bloody nose

_____ 8. **A:** Does your head feel hot?

    B: Yes. I have a _____ .

       a. bruise

       b. fever

       c. blister

       d. swollen finger

_____ 9. **A:** Does your stomach hurt?

    B: Yes. I always _____ on airplanes.

       a. feel nauseous

       b. sneeze

       c. cough

       d. feel dizzy

Complete the sentence.

10.   I feel sick. I have a _____ .

Illnesses and Medical Conditions

Name _____ Date _____

Write T (true) or F (false).

_____ 1. HIV (human immunodeficiency virus) causes AIDS.

_____ 2. Heart disease spreads through the air or water.

Choose the best answer.

_____ 3. I have a pain on the side of my head. I think I have _____.
   a. an ear infection
   b. intestinal parasites
   c. TB (tuberculosis)
   d. asthma

_____ 4. The doctor is checking for _____.
   a. strep throat
   b. cancer
   c. high blood pressure
   d. diabetes

_____ 5. Which is NOT a common illness?
   a. a cold
   b. an ear infection
   c. diabetes
   d. the flu

_____ 6. Which makes it hard to breathe?
   a. an ear infection
   b. asthma
   c. HIV (human immunodeficiency virus)
   d. intestinal parasites

_____ 7. _____ gives you spots on your skin.
   a. Strep throat
   b. Asthma
   c. Chicken pox
   d. Hypertension

_____ 8. Cats make me sneeze. I have _____.

      a. measles

      b. allergies

      c. diabetes

      d. chicken pox

Complete the dialogue.

_____ 9. **A:** How do you feel?

      B: I have a fever and my whole body hurts. I think I have _____.

      a. the flu

      b. arthritis

      c. diabetes

      d. heart disease

_____ 10. **A:** That is a bad cough, and your nose is red. Are you OK?

      B: No. I have _____.

      a. chicken pox

      b. an ear infection

      c. a cold

      d. intestinal parasites

A Pharmacy

Name _____ Date _____

Write T (true) or F (false).

_____ 1. A prescription label tells you about your medication.

Choose the best answer.

_____ 2. Which medication makes your eyes feel better?
   a. antacid
   b. eye drops
   c. nasal spray
   d. inhaler

_____ 3. Doctor, I feel very sick. Can you please write me a _____ for some medicine?
   a. prescription
   b. prescription label
   c. warning label
   d. dosage

_____ 4. The dosage is one _____ every four hours.
   a. cast
   b. cream
   c. cane
   d. capsule

_____ 5. I have a headache. I need _____.
   a. antacids
   b. a pain reliever
   c. nasal spray
   d. ointment

_____ 6. Take _____ for your stomachache.
   a. ointment
   b. cough syrup
   c. antacids
   d. vitamins

_____ 7. You take _____ with a spoon.
   a. an inhaler
   b. throat lozenges
   c. cough syrup
   d. eye drops

Complete the dialogue.

_____ 8. A: I need more of these capsules.
   B: OK. I need the _____ first.
   a. warning label
   b. prescription number
   c. expiration date
   d. dosage

_____ 9. A: I have a bad cold. I can't breathe through my nose.
   B: Do you want some _____?
   a. eye drops
   b. nasal spray
   c. throat lozenges
   d. cough syrup

Complete the sentence.

10. A person who sells prescription medication is a _____.

Medical Care

Name _____ Date _____

Write T (true) or F (false).

_____ **1.** A nurse can check your blood pressure.

_____ **2.** The doctor is examining the patient's throat.

_____ **3.** The receptionist can help you make an appointment.

_____ **4.** A doctor gives a patient a health insurance card.

Choose the best answer.

_____ **5.** The doctor is _____.
   a. examining the girl's throat
   b. listening to the girl's heart
   c. taking the girl's temperature
   d. checking the girl's blood pressure

Complete the dialogue.

_____ **6. A:** Is the doctor going to _____?
   B: Yes. He needs a blood sample.
   a. listen to my heart
   b. draw my blood
   c. examine my eyes
   d. take my temperature

_____ **7. A:** I'm here for my appointment.
   B: Please sit down and fill out this _____ first.
   a. health history form
   b. appointment
   c. syringe
   d. health insurance card

_____ **8. A:** Excuse me. Do you work here in the hospital?

   B: Oh, no. I'm a _____ . I'm waiting to see the doctor.
   - **a.** doctor
   - **b.** nurse
   - **c.** patient
   - **d.** receptionist

_____ **9. A:** My forehead feels hot.

   B: Let me _____ .
   - **a.** listen to your heart
   - **b.** draw some blood
   - **c.** examine your eyes
   - **d.** take your temperature

Complete the sentence.

10. This woman helps take care of sick people.

She is a _____ .

Name _____ Date _____

Write T (true) or F (false).

_____ **1.** Braces make teeth straight.

_____ **2.** Keep your teeth clean to stop decay.

Choose the best answer.

_____ **3.** To see inside your teeth, we need to _____.
   a. numb the mouth
   b. pull a tooth
   c. take x-rays
   d. fill a cavity

_____ **4.** There is a small hole in your tooth. We don't need to pull the tooth. We can
   _____ .
   a. fill the cavity
   b. clean your teeth
   c. take x-rays
   d. pull the tooth

_____ **5.** _____ helps a dentist fill cavities.
   a. A dental hygienist
   b. An orthodontist
   c. A dentist
   d. A dental assistant

_____ **6.** You should go to the dentist every six months to _____.
   a. pull your teeth
   b. drill your teeth
   c. clean your teeth
   d. numb your mouth

Complete the dialogue.

_____ **7.** **A:** What does this man have on his teeth?

B: He has _____ . The dental hygienist can clean it.

a. dentures
b. a filling
c. braces
d. plaque

_____ **8.** **A:** Dr. Perez, my tooth hurts!

B: I see a hole in your tooth. You have _____ .

a. a cavity
b. plaque
c. a filling
d. braces

_____ **9.** **A:** You have some decay.

B: Do I need to come back for _____ ?

a. dentures
b. a filling
c. braces
d. plaque

Complete the sentence.

10. The man with a mask is drilling a tooth.

He is a _____ .

The Bank

Name _____   Date _____

Write T (true) or F (false).

_____ 1. *Withdraw cash* means to put cash in your bank account.

_____ 2. A teller fixes ATMs.

Choose the best answer.

_____ 3. Chandni keeps her checks in _____.
   a. a passbook
   b. a check book
   c. a bank statement
   d. an ATM card

_____ 4. The number at the bottom of your check is your _____.
   a. balance
   b. savings account number
   c. checking account number
   d. PIN

_____ 5. Jill can't buy a new sofa. Her _____ at the bank is too low.
   a. savings account number
   b. balance
   c. checking account number
   d. vault

Complete the dialogue.

_____ 6. **A:** That's great! You can withdraw cash any time.

B: Yes, it's very easy with this _____ .

　　a. bank statement
　　b. ATM card
　　c. deposit slip
　　d. safety deposit box

_____ 7. **A:** I'm worried. We don't have any mail from the bank.

B: Me, too. The _____ has a lot of important information on it. It has our name, address, account number, and balance.

　　a. ATM card
　　b. deposit slip
　　c. safety deposit box
　　d. bank statement

_____ 8. **A:** My money and my deposit slip are in the envelope.

B: Great! You can _____ a deposit at the ATM.

　　a. bank
　　b. remove
　　c. make
　　d. withdraw

_____ 9. **A:** This check is from Uncle Steve for my birthday.

B: That's nice! Now you can _____ the check.

　　a. enter
　　b. cash
　　c. insert
　　d. remove

Complete the sentence.

10. There is a _____ waiting in line at the bank.

Name _____ Date _____

Choose the best answer.

_____ **1.** The person who writes a book is the _____.
    a. title
    b. headline
    c. author
    d. library clerk

_____ **2.** A person who gets books at the library is _____.
    a. a library patron
    b. an author
    c. a library clerk
    d. a reference librarian

_____ **3.** Your book is NOT back on time. You need to _____.
    a. pay a late fine
    b. look for a book
    c. get a library card
    d. check out a book

_____ **4.** The name of a book is the _____.
    a. author
    b. novel
    c. title
    d. atlas

_____ **5.** I like to read with my baby. She likes _____.
    a. newspapers
    b. novels
    c. headlines
    d. picture books

Complete the dialogue.

_____ 6. **A:** I want to use the library. What should I do first?

      B: You need to _____ .

        a. return a book

        b. check out a book

        c. get a library card

        d. pay a late fine

_____ 7. **A:** Can you please help me? I need information about World War II.

      B: Yes, I can help you _____ .

        a. look for a book

        b. pay a late fine

        c. get a library card

        d. return a book

_____ 8. **A:** I want to check this out.

      B: Please _____ in two weeks.

        a. pay a late fine

        b. return the book

        c. look for the book

        d. get a library card

_____ 9. **A:** I found something I want to read.

      B: Go to the circulation desk to _____ .

        a. check out your book

        b. pay a late fine

        c. look for your book

        d. return your book

Complete the sentence.

10. This woman helps people check out and return books.

She is a library _____ .

Name _____ Date _____

Write T (true) or F (false).

_____ **1.** A letter carrier delivers mail to people.

_____ **2.** You can ask the postal clerk to help you mail a letter.

Choose the best answer.

_____ **3.** You need to _____ the envelope
to mail a letter.
   a. address
   b. deliver
   c. receive
   d. read

_____ **4.** My brother lives in another country. He writes _____ to me
every week.
   a. a package
   b. a letter
   c. an envelope
   d. a mailing address

_____ **5.** Mom, I need a _____ to mail this
letter. Do you have one?
   a. post card
   b. stamp
   c. post office box
   d. postmark

Complete the dialogue.

_____ 6. **A:** Sandy and John have a new baby.

        B: Wow, I need to mail a _____ to them.

          a. postmark

          b. greeting card

          c. stamp

          d. letter carrier

_____ 7. **A:** Why do you have that big box?

        B: I'm taking it to the post office. It's a _____ for my friend in Ohio.

          a. greeting card

          b. post card

          c. book of stamps

          d. package

_____ 8. **A:** Do you need only one stamp?

        B: No, I need more. Please buy a _____.

          a. package

          b. book of stamps

          c. post card

          d. letter

Complete the sentence.

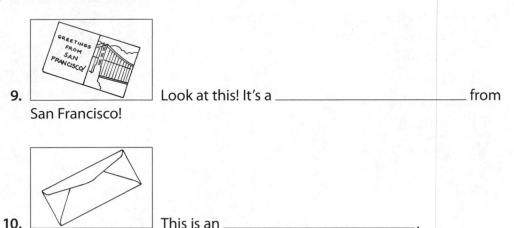

9. Look at this! It's a _____ from San Francisco!

10. This is an _____ .

Name _____ Date _____

Write T (true) or F (false).

_____ 1. You get your license before you get a learner's permit.

_____ 2. You get your license after passing a driving test.

Choose the best answer.

_____ 3. Which do you do first?
   a. get your license
   b. get a learner's permit
   c. pass a driving test
   d. take a written test

_____ 4. Rosa does NOT know how to drive. She wants to _____.
   a. take a written test
   b. take a driver education course
   c. pay the application fee
   d. show her identification

_____ 5. Jose is going to give the cashier $26.00. He is going to _____.
   a. study the handbook
   b. show his identification
   c. pay the application fee
   d. get his permit

_____ 6. I need your _____. Please put your thumb on the black pad.
   a. fingerprint
   b. vision exam
   c. photo
   d. DMV handbook

_____ 7. First, register your car. Then, put the _____ on your license plate.
   a. registration tag
   b. driver's license number
   c. proof of insurance
   d. expiration date

Complete the dialogue.

_____ 8. **A:** Where is the DMV clerk?

       B: You need to go to that _____.

          a. photo

          b. window

          c. fingerprint

          d. vision exam

_____ 9. **A:** Congratulations! You passed the driving test.

       B: Great! Now I have a _____.

          a. DMV handbook

          b. license plate

          c. driver's license

          d. fingerprint

_____ 10. **A:** Please tell me your _____.

       B: It's N57881049.

          a. expiration date

          b. registration sticker

          c. license plate

          d. driver's license number

_____ 11. **A:** What is that on the back of your car?

       B: It's _____.

          a. an expiration date

          b. a license plate

          c. a proof of insurance

          d. a driver's license number

Complete the sentence.

12. A person who works at the DMV is a _____.

13. The DMV clerk gives you a _____. It checks that you can see clearly.

14. I hope the _____ of me looks good on my driver's license.

15. The policy holder's name is on the proof of _____.

Government and Military Service

Name _____ Date _____

Write T (true) or F (false).

_____ **1.** The governor is the leader of a state.

_____ **2.** The mayor is the leader of a city.

_____ **3.** The state capital of Florida is Tallahassee.

Choose the best answer.

_____ **4.** The U.S. president lives in the _____ .
    a. Cabinet
    b. White House
    c. state capital
    d. Legislature

_____ **5.** The leader of the Executive Branch is _____ .
    a. the vice president
    b. the chief justice
    c. the president
    d. a congressperson

_____ **6.** The _____ is the leader of the Supreme Court.
    a. city council
    b. lieutenant governor
    c. chief justice
    d. president

_____ **7.** Which does NOT belong?
    a. a senator
    b. a congressperson
    c. a president
    d. the Supreme Court

_____ 8. The _____ is the Assembly and the State Senate.

     a. Legislature

     b. governor

     c. lieutenant governor

     d. House of Representatives

Complete the dialogue.

_____ 9. **A:** Who protects our country in the water?

     B: That is the _____.

     a. Army

     b. Navy

     c. chief justice

     d. Air Force

_____ 10. **A:** Who protects our country in the air?

     B: That is the _____.

     a. Army

     b. Navy

     c. Air Force

     d. Marines

Complete the sentence.

11. The branches of the Military are the _____, Navy, Air Force, Marines, Coast Guard, and National Guard.

12. The Senate and the House of Representatives make _____.

13. Congress works in the _____ building.

14. The mayor works with the _____ to make the city better.

15. Mary Jane is in the city council. She is a _____.

Public Safety

Name _____ Date _____

Write T (true) or F (false).

_____ 1. You lock your doors to protect your home.

Choose the best answer.

_____ 2. Roger walks home after he has two beers. Which public safety rule is he following?
    a. Walk with a friend.
    b. Don't drink and drive.
    c. Stay on well-lit streets.
    d. Report suspicious packages.

_____ 3. You see someone commit a crime. You should _____.
    a. walk with a friend
    b. conceal your PIN number
    c. report the crime to the police
    d. shop on secure websites

_____ 4. It is dark after work. Kathleen should _____.
    a. report suspicious packages
    b. conceal her PIN number
    c. walk with a friend
    d. shop on secure websites

Complete the dialogue.

_____ 5. **A:** I am going on a trip. How can I keep my money safe?
    B: You should _____.
    a. protect your purse or wallet
    b. report suspicious packages
    c. join a Neighborhood Watch
    d. report crimes to the police

_____ **6. A:** I am home alone. How can I be safe?

      B: _____ .

          a. Don't open your door to strangers.

          b. Don't drink and drive.

          c. Stay on well-lit streets.

          d. Be aware of your surroundings.

_____ **7. A:** I am going to buy my books on the Internet.

      B: Make sure you _____ .

          a. stay on well-lit streets

          b. shop on secure websites

          c. are aware of your surroundings

          d. join a Neighborhood Watch

_____ **8. A:** This is John. He lives in the house next to me.

      B: Would he like to _____ ?

          a. lock his doors

          b. shop on secure websites

          c. join our Neighborhood Watch

          d. report suspicious packages

_____ **9. A:** I need books for school, but I don't have cash.

      B: Use your bank card, but make sure you _____ .

          a. stay on well-lit streets

          b. conceal your PIN number

          c. join a Neighborhood Watch

          d. lock your doors

_____ **10. A:** Is this a safe neighborhood for shopping?

      B: Yes, but you should always _____ .

          a. shop on secure websites

          b. report suspicious packages

          c. join a Neighborhood Watch

          d. be aware of your surroundings

Emergency Procedures

Name _____ Date _____

Write T (true) or F (false).

_____ 1. You should NOT follow directions during an emergency.

_____ 2. You should NOT watch the weather during an emergency.

_____ 3. Pay attention to warnings. Watch TV and listen to the radio.

Choose the best answer.

_____ 4. During an emergency, it is important to _____.
   a. remain calm
   b. plan for an emergency
   c. make a disaster kit
   d. inspect utilities

_____ 5. There are trees and broken windows on the ground. We need to go outside and _____.
   a. take cover
   b. evacuate the area
   c. clean up the debris
   d. inspect the utilities

_____ 6. After an emergency, we need to _____.
   a. inspect the utilities
   b. take cover
   c. watch the weather
   d. make a disaster kit

_____ 7. Someone is hurt. Use the _____.
   a. first aid kit
   b. toilet paper
   c. flashlight
   d. batteries

_____ 8. Before an emergency, you should _____ .

    a. take cover

    b. evacuate the area

    c. make a disaster kit

    d. stay away from windows

Complete the dialogue.

_____ 9. **A:** We need lots of _____ .

    B: OK. I am putting sweaters and jackets in the disaster kit.

    a. moist towelettes

    b. warm clothes

    c. cash and coins

    d. batteries

_____ 10. **A:** Warm clothes are not enough at night.

    B: OK. Let's put _____ in the disaster kit, too.

    a. cash and coins

    b. bottled water

    c. packaged food

    d. blankets

_____ 11. **A:** Can we put fresh fruit and vegetables in the disaster kit?

    B: No, it is better to have _____ to eat.

    a. canned food

    b. toilet paper

    c. batteries

    d. warm clothes

Complete the sentence.

12. There is no electricity. We need to use the _____ to see.

13. We need _____ for the flashlight.

14. Please have enough _____ for everyone to drink.

15. We need a _____ to open the canned food.

Name _____ Date _____

Write T (true) or F (false).

_____ **1.** This sign means *handicapped parking*.

_____ **2.** This sign means *no left turn*.

_____ **3.** This sign means *pedestrian crossing*.

Choose the best answer.

_____ **4.** Stop! The sign says _____.
    a. *do not enter*
    b. *U-turn OK*
    c. *merge*
    d. *speed limit 40*

_____ **5.** What does this sign mean?
    a. You have to stop.
    b. You have to turn left.
    c. There's a railroad crossing.
    d. You can only go one way.

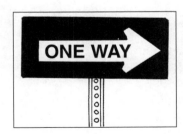

_____ **6.** You are driving too fast. The _____ is 35.
    a. speed limit
    b. U.S. route
    c. pedestrian crossing
    d. road work

_____ 7. We can't leave the car here. The sign says _____.

    a. *U-turn OK*

    b. *speed limit 25*

    c. *no parking*

    d. *right turn only*

Complete the dialogue.

_____ 8. **A:** Which way do I go?

    B: The sign says _____.

      a. *one way*

      b. *U-turn OK*

      c. *right turn only*

      d. *no left turn*

Complete the sentence.

9. This is the shape of a _____ sign.

10. A _____ sign means you should let other cars go first.

Directions and Maps

Name _____   Date _____

Write T (true) or F (false).

_____ 1. You can buy an Internet map at a gas station.

_____ 2. You use the scale on a map to find the miles between places.

Choose the best answer.

_____ 3. What does *go straight* mean?
   a. turn left
   b. right turn only
   c. stop
   d. do not turn

_____ 4. On a map, which direction is to the left?
   a. north
   b. south
   c. east
   d. west

_____ 5. This sign means that you should _____.
   a. stop
   b. turn left
   c. turn right
   d. go straight

_____ 6. On a map, _____ is at the top.
   a. north
   b. south
   c. east
   d. west

_____ 7. On a map, which direction is to the right?
   a. north
   b. south
   c. east
   d. west

Complete the dialogue.

_____ 8. **A:** Which way do I go?

   B: The sign says to _____.

    a. go straight

    b. stop

    c. turn right

    d. turn left

_____ 9. **A:** The traffic light is turning red.

   B: You should _____ at the corner.

    a. stop

    b. go

    c. turn left

    d. turn right

_____ 10. **A:** Where is Mexico?

   B: It is _____ of the United States.

    a. north

    b. south

    c. east

    d. west

Buying and Maintaining a Car

Name _____ Date _____

Write T (true) or F (false).

_____ **1.** You check the oil in this part of the car.

_____ **2.** You buy a car. The seller registers the car.

Choose the best answer.

_____ **3.** Your car won't start. What should you do?
    a. go for a smog check
    b. replace the windshield wipers
    c. fill the tires with air
    d. take the car to a mechanic

_____ **4.** You buy a car. Then you _____.
    a. look at car ads
    b. negotiate a price
    c. get the title from the seller
    d. ask the seller about the car

_____ **5.** You want to find a car. What should you do first?
    a. go for a smog check
    b. register the car
    c. get the title
    d. look at car ads

_____ **6.** Pablo checks his car radiator. Then he _____.
    a. puts in oil
    b. fills it with gas
    c. puts in coolant
    d. fills it with air

_____ **7.** Which do you do before you buy a car?

     a. get the title from the seller

     b. ask the seller about the car

     c. register the car

     d. fill the tank with gas

Complete the dialogue.

_____ **8.** **A:** The seller is asking $4,000 for the car, but I want to pay $3,500.

     B: Why don't you _____?

     a. negotiate the price

     b. get the title from the seller

     c. register the car

     d. ask the seller about the car

_____ **9.** **A:** What is this hole on the side of the car?

     B: You use it to _____.

     a. check the oil

     b. fill the tank with gas

     c. put in coolant

     d. fill the tires with air

_____ **10.** **A:** Black smoke is coming from the back of my car.

     B: You should _____.

     a. go for a smog check

     b. fill the tires with air

     c. fill the tank with gas

     d. replace the windshield wipers

Name _____ Date _____

Write T (true) or F (false).

_____ 1. This man works in an office.

_____ 2. A pay stub shows an employee's deductions.

Choose the best answer.

_____ 3. She answers the phones in the office. She
is the _____.
   a. supervisor
   b. payroll clerk
   c. receptionist
   d. customer

_____ 4. Kate works for Town Bank. She is _____ of Town Bank.
   a. an employer
   b. a supervisor
   c. a customer
   d. an employee

_____ 5. This picture shows the _____ the
post office.
   a. time clock at
   b. entrance to
   c. supervisor of
   d. safety regulations for

_____ 6. Lila writes the paychecks for the workers at her office.
She is the _____.
   a. receptionist
   b. customer
   c. employee
   d. payroll clerk

_____ 7. Andy's _____ are $600 a month.
- **a.** payroll clerks
- **b.** time clocks
- **c.** wages
- **d.** safety regulations

Complete the dialogue.

_____ 8. **A:** Do you work for Mr. Babic?

B: No. Mr. Babic works for me. I am his _____ .
- **a.** receptionist
- **b.** employer
- **c.** customer
- **d.** payroll clerk

_____ 9. **A:** Why are we going to the bank?

B: I need to take my _____ there.
- **a.** paycheck
- **b.** deductions
- **c.** time clock
- **d.** receptionist

Complete the sentence.

10. A _____ shows the time an employee starts and finishes work.

Name _____   Date _____

Write T (true) or F (false).

_____ **1.** This woman is taking dictation.

_____ **2.** You can staple papers together.

Choose the best answer.

_____ **3.** You can use this to _____ .
- **a.** type a letter
- **b.** scan a document
- **c.** check messages
- **d.** transfer a call

_____ **4.** You are working on your computer. You want a copy of your document.
You can _____ it.
- **a.** transcribe
- **b.** print
- **c.** organize
- **d.** transfer

_____ **5.** Joe _____ on his computer.
- **a.** enters data
- **b.** collates papers
- **c.** leaves a message
- **d.** greets a caller

Complete the dialogue.

_____ 6. **A:** Were there any calls for me?

 B: I don't know. Why don't you _____?
  a. scan a document
  b. organize your materials
  c. schedule a meeting
  d. check your messages

_____ 7. **A:** Hello. Can I talk to Sue Jones?

 B: She isn't here. Do you want to _____?
  a. put the caller on hold
  b. take a message
  c. leave a message
  d. greet the caller

_____ 8. **A:** Can I speak with Joan?

 B: I'm sorry. She's not here. Can I _____?
  a. leave a message
  b. take a message
  c. fax a document
  d. scan a document

Complete the sentence.

9. I need to show this to everyone in the meeting.

Please _____ of it.

10. Micah wants to read this letter now.

Please _____ it to him.

Name _____ Date _____

Write T (true) or F (false).

_____ 1. You get vocational training at a job fair.

_____ 2. Training can help you get a better job.

Choose the best answer.

_____ 3. You can learn about different jobs _____.
  a. in on-the-job training
  b. at a job fair
  c. in an entry-level job
  d. in an online course

_____ 4. You want to plan your career. A _____ can help you.
  a. new job
  b. promotion
  c. recruiter
  d. career counselor

_____ 5. Which is a kind of training?
  a. internship
  b. job fair
  c. skill inventory
  d. promotion

_____ 6. Sofia is going to have a higher-level job. She still works for the same company. She is getting _____.
  a. an online course
  b. an entry-level job
  c. a promotion
  d. an internship

Complete the dialogue.

_____ 7. **A:** How can I learn more at my job?

    B: Get _____ .

      a. an entry-level job

      b. on-the-job training

      c. a recruiter

      d. a skill inventory

_____ 8. **A:** I need help planning my career.

    B: You can go to _____ .

      a. vocational training

      b. an entry-level job

      c. an online course

      d. a resource center

_____ 9. **A:** Are you a supervisor at this store?

    B: No, I am a clerk. I have _____ .

      a. an entry-level job

      b. a promotion

      c. a new job

      d. a career counselor

_____ 10. **A:** Do you work at ABC Company?

    B: Yes, but I am looking for _____ . I want to work with children.

      a. a promotion

      b. a new job

      c. an entry-level job

      d. a recruiter

Name _____ Date _____

Write T (true) or F (false).

_____ **1.** You can look in the classifieds for a job.

_____ **2.** You write a cover letter after a job interview.

Choose the best answer.

_____ **3.** First, send in your resume. Then, _____.
   a. look in the classifieds
   b. write a cover letter
   c. set up an interview
   d. network

_____ **4.** You can _____ to learn more about a job.
   a. fill out an application
   b. go on an interview
   c. get hired
   d. look for a help wanted sign

_____ **5.** The company likes you. You are going
   to _____.
   a. network
   b. fill out an application
   c. go to an employment agency
   d. get hired

_____ **6.** You _____ to describe your jobs and education.
   a. get hired
   b. write a resume
   c. talk to friends
   d. look in the classifieds

_____ **7.** You are looking for a job. You can use a computer to _____.
   a. get hired
   b. look for help wanted signs
   c. go to an employment agency
   d. check Internet job sites

Complete the dialogue.

_____ 8. **A:** There is a help wanted sign at the movie theater.

       B: Go and _____ right now!

        a. look in the classifieds

        b. fill out an application

        c. talk to friends

        d. check Internet job sites

_____ 9. **A:** How do I look for a job?

       B: First, _____ .

        a. get hired

        b. talk to friends

        c. fill out an application

        d. set up an interview

_____ 10. **A:** I'm looking at the classifieds. I don't see any jobs. What can I do?

       B: You can _____ at the mall.

        a. get hired

        b. write a cover letter

        c. look for help wanted signs

        d. talk to friends

Interview Skills

Name _____ Date _____

Write T (true) or F (false).

_____ 1. You should turn off your cell phone in the middle of an interview.

_____ 2. Don't be late to an interview. You may not get the job.

Choose the best answer.

_____ 3. The interviewer is talking during a job interview. What should you do?
a. turn off your cell phone
b. greet the interviewer
c. write a thank-you note
d. listen carefully

_____ 4. You should learn more about the company to _____.
a. talk about your experience
b. prepare for the interview
c. be neat
d. listen carefully

_____ 5. Which should you do after an interview?
a. write a thank-you note
b. bring your resume and ID
c. turn off your cell phone
d. prepare for the interview

Complete the dialogue.

_____ 6. **A:** This job at the bank sounds good. But I can't work in the mornings.

     B: Remember, you can _____ at the job interview.

       a. dress appropriately

       b. thank the interviewer

       c. ask questions

       d. write a thank-you note

_____ 7. **A:** Should I wear shorts to my job interview?

     B: No! You need to _____.

       a. prepare for the interview

       b. talk about your experience

       c. dress appropriately

       d. be on time

_____ 8. **A:** I have an interview tomorrow. Do I need anything?

     B: Yes. You should bring _____.

       a. your resume and ID

       b. your cell phone

       c. a thank-you note

       d. a friend

_____ 9. **A:** I have an interview today.

     B: Comb your hair. You need to _____.

       a. be neat

       b. dress appropriately

       c. shake hands

       d. make eye contact

Complete the sentence.

10. _____ You should _____ at the interview.

Job Safety

Name _____ Date _____

Write T (true) or F (false).

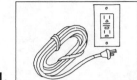

_____ 1. This is a frayed cord.

_____ 2. Broken equipment is a safety hazard.

Choose the best answer.

_____ 3. Which does NOT belong?
    a. broken equipment
    b. slippery floor
    c. careful worker
    d. frayed cord

_____ 4. Which does NOT go on your head?
    a. safety visor
    b. earmuffs
    c. hard hat
    d. knee pads

_____ 5. There are loud noises at work. Wear _____.
    a. a safety visor
    b. work gloves
    c. a hard hat
    d. ear plugs

_____ 6. The safety hazard in this picture is _____.
    a. a slippery floor
    b. broken equipment
    c. flammable liquids
    d. radioactive materials

Complete the dialogue.

_____ 7. **A:** Richard isn't wearing a hard hat.

    B: I know. He is _____.

      a. poisonous

      b. a careless worker

      c. radioactive

      d. a careful worker

_____ 8. **A:** Bendak builds houses. How does he protect his feet?

    B: He wears _____.

      a. knee pads

      b. safety boots

      c. safety goggles

      d. safety glasses

_____ 9. **A:** Look! I see smoke!

    B: Quick! Give me the _____.

      a. particle mask

      b. ear plugs

      c. fire extinguisher

      d. work gloves

Complete the sentence.

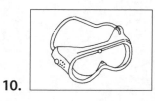

10. Protect your eyes. Put on your _____.

An Office

Name _____ Date _____

Write T (true) or F (false).

_____ 1. A scanner sends packages.

_____ 2. You can type letters with a stapler.

_____ 3. You put paper in a laser printer.

Choose the best answer.

_____ 4. You put file folders in a _____.
   a. rotary card file
   b. paper cutter
   c. photocopier
   d. file cabinet

_____ 5. Which has walls?
   a. an executive
   b. letterhead
   c. a PBX
   d. a cubicle

_____ 6. A _____ holds papers together.
   a. paper clip
   b. mailing label
   c. calculator
   d. paper cutter

_____ 7. Which person fixes things in an office?
   a. a receptionist
   b. a file clerk
   c. a computer technician
   d. an executive

Complete the dialogue.

_____ 8. **A:** Where is our meeting?

B: It's in the _____.
  - **a.** cubicle
  - **b.** conference room
  - **c.** reception area
  - **d.** waiting area

_____ 9. **A:** Do we have any sticky notes?

B: Yes. They are in the _____.
  - **a.** supply cabinet
  - **b.** paper shredder
  - **c.** organizer
  - **d.** envelope

Complete the sentence.

10.  We need ten of these letters.

Please use the _____.

Name _____ Date _____

Write T (true) or F (false).

_____ 1. A doorman opens and closes the front doors in a hotel.

_____ 2. The concierge at a hotel parks your car.

Choose the best answer.

_____ 3. Who helps you with your luggage?
    a. a housekeeper
    b. a guest
    c. a desk clerk
    d. a bellhop

_____ 4. You pay for your hotel room at the _____.
    a. luggage cart
    b. gift shop
    c. revolving door
    d. front desk

_____ 5. A _____ cleans the hotel rooms.
    a. doorman
    b. bell captain
    c. housekeeper
    d. desk clerk

_____ 6. You sleep in a _____.
    a. guest room
    b. hallway
    c. meeting room
    d. ballroom

_____ 7. A _____ helps guests with their cars.
    a. bell captain
    b. desk clerk
    c. parking attendant
    d. housekeeper

_____ 8. A _____ works at the front desk of a hotel.
   a. doorman
   b. housekeeper
   c. bell captain
   d. desk clerk

Complete the dialogue.

_____ 9. **A:** Where are my bags?

   B: They are _____.
   a. on the housekeeping cart
   b. on the luggage cart
   c. in the gift shop
   d. in the ballroom

_____ 10. **A:** Do you want to eat in the hotel restaurant?

   B: No. I want to call _____.
   a. a bellhop
   b. room service
   c. pool service
   d. a housekeeper

English Composition

Name _____ Date _____

Write T (true) or F (false).

_____ 1. A paragraph is a group of sentences about one thing.

_____ 2. You write a final draft. Then you revise it.

Choose the best answer.

_____ 3. Which punctuation is between the words *scared* and *but* in this sentence?
   a. colon
   b. semicolon
   c. comma
   d. period

> *I was homesick and scared, but I did not go home.*

_____ 4. This is an example of a _____ .
   a. sentence
   b. quotation
   c. paragraph
   d. comma

> *My first job wasn't good.*

_____ 5. _____ means to look for mistakes in your paper.
   a. *Turn in your paper*
   b. *Edit*
   c. *Write a first draft*
   d. *Revise*

_____ 6. The punctuation at the end of this sentence shows a strong feeling. It is _____ .
   a. an exclamation mark
   b. a comma
   c. an apostrophe
   d. a question mark

> *I believed in my future success!*

_____ 7. Don't forget to put a _____ at the end of a sentence.

    a. comma

    b. hyphen

    c. semicolon

    d. period

Complete the dialogue.

_____ 8. **A:** I am organizing my ideas now.

    B: Good. Next, you can _____ .

    a. proofread your paper

    b. revise your paper

    c. write a first draft

    d. turn in your paper

_____ 9. **A:** Please spell your last name.

    B: It's O'Conner. O- _____ -C-O-N-N-E-R.

    a. period

    b. apostrophe

    c. quotation mark

    d. semicolon

Complete the sentence.

10. In this sentence, _____
show the exact words of Henry David Thoreau.

> Henry David Thoreau said,
> "Men are born to succeed,
> not fail."

Science

Name _____   Date _____

Write T (true) or F (false).

_____ 1. A chemist studies animals.

_____ 2. An atom and a basketball are the same size.

_____ 3. A test tube can hold water.

_____ 4. A molecule is a scientist.

_____ 5. Organisms are NOT alive.

_____ 6. All living things have cells.

Choose the best answer.

_____ 7. A person who studies animals is a _____.
    a. physicist
    b. Bunsen burner
    c. biologist
    d. beaker

_____ 8. We look through the _____ of a microscope.
    a. light source
    b. arm
    c. base
    d. eyepiece

_____ 9. Hoshiko is mixing the liquids in a _____.
    a. dropper
    b. funnel
    c. beaker
    d. prism

_____ 10. Mena heats the water with a _____.
    a. Bunsen burner
    b. proton
    c. magnet
    d. funnel

_____ 11. You can carry a microscope by its _____.

     a. stage clips

     b. arm

     c. revolving nosepiece

     d. fine adjustment knob

Complete the dialogue.

_____ 12. **A:** Let's look at this under the microscope.

     B: Put it on the _____.

     a. stage

     b. base

     c. prism

     d. magnet

_____ 13. **A:** How many elements are there?

     B: I'm not sure. Look at the _____.

     a. balance

     b. periodic table

     c. cell wall

     d. objective

_____ 14. **A:** How can I look at a drop of water under the microscope?

     B: First, you put it _____.

     a. in a beaker

     b. on a slide

     c. in a test tube

     d. on a balance

Complete the sentence.

15. Protons, neutrons, and electrons are in the _____ of an atom.

Computers

Name _____ Date _____

Write T (true) or F (false).

_____ 1. The hard drive is inside your computer.

_____ 2. We delete incorrect words and letters.

Choose the best answer.

_____ 3. My _____ is broken. I can't put this letter on paper.
  a. keyboard
  b. printer
  c. tower
  d. webcam

_____ 4. Many parts of a computer are inside the _____.
  a. software
  b. surge protector
  c. tower
  d. mouse

Complete the dialogue.

_____ 5. A: How do you draw pictures on the computer?
  B: I have _____ for that.
  a. a motherboard
  b. a microprocessor
  c. a webcam
  d. software

_____ 6. A: Let's watch a movie or listen to music on your computer.
  B: We can't. My computer doesn't have a _____.
  a. keyboard
  b. mouse
  c. DVD and CD-ROM drive
  d. tower

_____ 7. **A:** How do I close this program?

        B: Use the _____ .

          a. USB port

          b. tower

          c. screen

          d. mouse

_____ 8. **A:** What's wrong with your computer?

        B: The _____ is broken.

          a. monitor

          b. DVD and CD-ROM drive

          c. flash drive

          d. printer

_____ 9. **A:** How do I make a word or letter blue on the screen?

        B: First, _____ with the mouse.

          a. type it

          b. select it

          c. delete it

          d. go to the next line

Complete the sentence.

10. I can't find the letter "Q" on the _____ .

The Internet

Name _____ Date _____

Write T (true) or F (false).

_____ 1. The pointer is often a small arrow.

_____ 2. The back button shows you the back of a webpage.

_____ 3. The menu bar lists menus. Some examples are File, Edit, View, History, Bookmarks, and Tools.

Choose the best answer.

_____ 4. Many webpages have a _____ on the right side. You can use it to go up and down the page.
   a. tab
   b. menu bar
   c. website address
   d. scroll bar

_____ 5. Which should you do after checking the spelling in your email?
   a. send the email
   b. type your password
   c. click "sign in"
   d. type the message

_____ 6. _____ in this big box under the subject line.
   a. Click "sign in"
   b. Type the message
   c. Send the email
   d. Attach a picture

Complete the dialogue.

_____ 7. **A:** What is that flashing line in the text box?

B: Oh, that's the _____ . You can type there.

    a. cursor

    b. tab

    c. text box

    d. URL

_____ 8. **A:** What do I put in this text box? It's the box that says _To:_

B: That's where you _____ . Who are you sending the message to?

    a. type your password

    b. address the email

    c. type the subject

    d. attach a file

_____ 9. **A:** What's the _____ of the news website?

B: It's http://www.news4you.us.

    a. cursor

    b. search engine

    c. URL

    d. forward button

_____ 10. **A:** My username and password are there. Now what do I do?

B: _____

    a. Click "sign in."

    b. Type the message.

    c. Send the email.

    d. Address the email.

Name _____ Date _____

Write T (true) or F (false).

_____ 1. Native Americans are from Europe.

_____ 2. A Bill of Rights is a receipt for things you buy in a store.

_____ 3. The Revolutionary War was between the United States and England.

_____ 4. In the Colonial Period, there were slaves in the United States.

_____ 5. The colonists did NOT live in Virginia, New Jersey, Pennsylvania, or Rhode Island.

Choose the best answer.

_____ 6. The first words of the _____ are "We the people."
   a. Bill of Rights
   b. Declaration of Independence
   c. First Continental Congress
   d. Constitution

_____ 7. The _____ were the creators of the United States.
   a. founders
   b. colonists
   c. minutemen
   d. redcoats

_____ 8. The _____ is an important document.
   a. Revolutionary War
   b. First Continental Congress
   c. Native American
   d. Declaration of Independence

_____ 9. George Washington was the first _____ of the United States.
   a. president
   b. minuteman
   c. redcoat
   d. slave

_____ **10.** New York and Georgia were two of the _____.

    a. thirteen colonies

    b. colonists

    c. founders

    d. Native Americans

Energy and Conservation

Name _____   Date _____

Write T (true) or F (false).

_____ **1.** Solar energy is from the sun.

_____ **2.** Natural gas is NOT an energy source.

_____ **3.** Water makes nuclear energy.

_____ **4.** Wind power is an energy source.

_____ **5.** People can carpool to conserve energy and resources.

Choose the best answer.

_____ **6.** Cars and factories make _____ .
    a. natural gas
    b. air pollution
    c. solar energy
    d. radiation

_____ **7.** Which is NOT an energy source?
    a. wind
    b. hazardous waste
    c. coal
    d. oil

_____ **8.** _____ is a liquid.
    a. Radiation
    b. Wind
    c. Oil
    d. Coal

_____ **9.** We find _____ under the ground.
    a. wind
    b. solar energy
    c. nuclear energy
    d. coal

_____ 10. No one is in the kitchen. Please _____ the lights.

     a. reuse

     b. recycle

     c. turn off

     d. compost

_____ 11. Please _____ . It makes the streets dirty.

     a. use energy-efficient bulbs

     b. adjust the thermostat

     c. carpool

     d. don't litter

Complete the dialogue.

_____ 12. **A:** I don't see any fish in this lake!

     B: The _____ in the lake is terrible.

     a. water pollution

     b. air pollution

     c. geothermal energy

     d. solar energy

_____ 13. **A:** Do you turn off the water when you brush your teeth?

     B: Yes, I always try to _____ water.

     a. reduce

     b. recycle

     c. save

     d. compost

_____ 14. **A:** Don't put the empty bottles and cans in the trash!

     B: You're right. We can _____ them.

     a. fix

     b. reduce

     c. adjust

     d. recycle

_____ 15. **A:** Should we buy paper plates?

     B: No. We can't wash them. We need to _____ trash.

     a. carpool

     b. save

     c. reduce

     d. adjust

Name _____ Date _____

Write T (true) or F (false).

_____ 1. There are animals at the zoo.

_____ 2. You see fish at a classical concert.

Choose the best answer.

_____ 3. The people are walking around the _____.
   a. art museum
   b. zoo
   c. amusement park
   d. flea market

_____ 4. The children are at the _____.
   a. movies
   b. amusement park
   c. county fair
   d. aquarium

_____ 5. Mohammed wants to buy a quilt at the _____.
   a. classical concert
   b. bowling alley
   c. opera
   d. county fair

_____ 6. What a beautiful _____!
   a. botanical garden
   b. nightclub
   c. county fair
   d. bowling alley

_____ 7. People watch actors in _____.
   a. zoos
   b. plays
   c. nightclubs
   d. bowling alleys

_____ **8.** You use a heavy ball at a _____.

    a. movie

    b. nightclub

    c. bowling alley

    d. swap meet

_____ **9.** There are musicians and actors on stage at the _____.

    a. zoo

    b. aquarium

    c. art museum

    d. opera

Complete the sentence.

10. Everybody's at the _____.

Entertainment

Name _____ Date _____

Write T (true) or F (false).

_____ 1. A soap opera is a TV program about soap.

_____ 2. Dramas are serious.

Choose the best answer.

_____ 3. Which type of TV program is funny?
   a. sitcom (situation comedy)
   b. drama
   c. sports program
   d. news program

_____ 4. Which type of TV program tells you important information?
   a. cartoon
   b. sitcom (situation comedy)
   c. soap opera
   d. news program

_____ 5. A good _____ has a lot of adventure.
   a. tragedy
   b. comedy
   c. romance
   d. action story

_____ 6. There are real people and no actors in a _____.
   a. sitcom (situation comedy)
   b. comedy
   c. horror story
   d. reality show

_____ 7. Which is a kind of movie?
   a. mystery
   b. soap opera
   c. R&B
   d. reggae

Complete the dialogue.

_____ 8. **A:** Do you like to watch football on TV?

B: Yes, I like all kinds of _____.

    a. mysteries

    b. dramas

    c. action stories

    d. sports programs

_____ 9. **A:** What kind of music do you like?

B: My favorite is _____ music. I like to watch music videos on TV and dance.

    a. jazz

    b. world

    c. pop

    d. classical

Complete the sentence.

10. Another name for R&B music is _____.

Name _____   Date _____

Choose the best answer.

_____ 1. A _____ is a Halloween decoration. You can put a candle in it.
     a. jack-o'-lantern
     b. mask
     c. candy cane
     d. parade

_____ 2. That _____ on his face is scary.
     a. candy
     b. mask
     c. turkey
     d. candy cane

_____ 3. There are many people in a _____ .
     a. card
     b. costume
     c. flag
     d. parade

_____ 4. Are you coming to the big _____ on Thanksgiving? There's going
to be a lot to eat.
     a. turkey
     b. costume
     c. ornament
     d. feast

_____ 5. When are you going to put on that funny _____?
     a. float
     b. heart
     c. costume
     d. candy

_____ **6.** Every country has a _____. The one for the United States is red, white, and blue.

    a. mask

    b. parade

    c. heart

    d. flag

_____ **7.** A _____ is tall and green. It has string lights and ornaments on it.

    a. heart

    b. flag

    c. Christmas tree

    d. candy cane

_____ **8.** _____ can be very dangerous.

    a. Fireworks

    b. Confetti

    c. Couples

    d. Cards

Complete the dialogue.

_____ **9. A:** Are you going to the parade?

    B: Yes, I am. I like to see the _____.

    a. turkeys

    b. hearts

    c. floats

    d. string lights

_____ **10. A:** I'm making this _____ in art class.

    B: It's beautiful. You should put it on your Christmas tree.

    a. mask

    b. costume

    c. float

    d. ornament

Answer Key

Personal Information, pp. 1–2

1. **ANSWER:** B
   REFERENCE: OPD, Personal Information, p. 4
   OBJECTIVE: Respond appropriately to common personal information questions
   STANDARD: CASAS 0.2.1
   OPD TERM: phone number

2. **ANSWER:** A
   REFERENCE: OPD, Personal Information, p. 4
   OBJECTIVE: Complete a personal information form
   STANDARD: CASAS 0.2.2
   OPD TERM: address

3. **ANSWER:** B
   REFERENCE: OPD, Personal Information, p. 4
   OBJECTIVE: Complete a personal information form
   STANDARD: CASAS 0.2.2
   OPD TERM: sign your name

4. **ANSWER:** B
   REFERENCE: OPD, Personal Information, p. 4
   OBJECTIVE: Respond appropriately to common personal information questions
   STANDARD: CASAS 0.2.1
   OPD TERM: name

5. **ANSWER:** A
   REFERENCE: OPD, Personal Information, p. 4
   OBJECTIVE: Complete a personal information form
   STANDARD: CASAS 0.2.2
   OPD TERM: city

6. **ANSWER:** B
   REFERENCE: OPD, Personal Information, p. 4
   OBJECTIVE: Complete a personal information form
   STANDARD: CASAS 0.2.2
   OPD TERM: state

7. **ANSWER:** C
   REFERENCE: OPD, Personal Information, p. 4
   OBJECTIVE: Respond appropriately to common personal information questions
   STANDARD: CASAS 0.2.1
   OPD TERM: ZIP code

8. **ANSWER:** C
   REFERENCE: OPD, Personal Information, p. 4
   OBJECTIVE: Respond appropriately to common personal information questions
   STANDARD: CASAS 0.2.1
   OPD TERM: spell your name

9. **ANSWER:** A
   REFERENCE: OPD, Personal Information, p. 4
   OBJECTIVE: Respond appropriately to common personal information questions
   STANDARD: CASAS 0.2.1
   OPD TERM: date of birth

10. **ANSWER:** sex
    REFERENCE: OPD, Personal Information, p. 4
    OBJECTIVE: Complete a personal information form
    STANDARD: CASAS 0.2.2
    OPD TERM: sex

Studying, pp. 3–4

1. **ANSWER:** T
   REFERENCE: OPD, Studying, pp. 8–9
   OBJECTIVE: Identify or utilize effective study strategies
   STANDARD: CASAS 7.4.1
   OPD TERM: put away your books

2. **ANSWER:** B
   REFERENCE: OPD, Studying, pp. 8–9
   OBJECTIVE: Identify or use appropriate classroom behavior
   STANDARD: CASAS 0.1.5
   OPD TERM: share a book

3. **ANSWER:** A
   REFERENCE: OPD, Studying, pp. 8–9
   OBJECTIVE: Identify or use appropriate classroom behavior
   STANDARD: CASAS 0.1.5
   OPD TERM: draw a picture

4. **ANSWER:** B
   REFERENCE: OPD, Studying, pp. 8–9
   OBJECTIVE: Identify or utilize test-taking skills
   STANDARD: CASAS 7.4.7
   OPD TERM: choose the correct answer

5. **ANSWER:** C
   REFERENCE: OPD, Studying, pp. 8–9
   OBJECTIVE: Identify or use appropriate classroom behavior
   STANDARD: CASAS 0.1.5
   OPD TERM: copy the word

6. **ANSWER:** B
   REFERENCE: OPD, Studying, pp. 8–9
   OBJECTIVE: Identify or use appropriate classroom behavior
   STANDARD: CASAS 0.1.5
   OPD TERM: take out a piece of paper

7. **ANSWER:** A
   REFERENCE: OPD, Studying, pp. 8–9
   OBJECTIVE: Identify or use appropriate classroom behavior
   STANDARD: CASAS 0.1.5
   OPD TERM: ask a question

8. **ANSWER:** C
   REFERENCE: OPD, Studying, pp. 8–9
   OBJECTIVE: Identify a problem and its possible causes
   STANDARD: CASAS 7.3.1
   OPD TERM: discuss a problem

9. **ANSWER:** A
   REFERENCE: OPD, Studying, pp. 8–9
   OBJECTIVE: Devise and implement a solution to an identified problem
   STANDARD: CASAS 7.3.2
   OPD TERM: brainstorm solutions

10. **ANSWER:** D
    REFERENCE: OPD, Studying, pp. 8–9
    OBJECTIVE: Demonstrate ability to work cooperatively with others as a member of a team, contributing to team efforts, maximizing the strengths of team members, promoting effective group interaction, and taking personal responsibility for accomplishing goals
    STANDARD: CASAS 4.8.1
    OPD TERM: work in a group

Succeeding in School, pp. 5–6

1. **ANSWER:** F
   REFERENCE: OPD, Succeeding in School, p. 10
   OBJECTIVE: Identify or use appropriate language for informational purposes (e.g., to identify, describe, ask for information, state needs, command, agree or disagree, ask permission)
   STANDARD: CASAS 0.1.2
   OPD TERM: pass a test

2. **ANSWER:** F
   REFERENCE: OPD, Succeeding in School, p. 10
   OBJECTIVE: Identify or utilize effective study strategies
   STANDARD: CASAS 7.4.1
   OPD TERM: study at home

3. **ANSWER:** D
   REFERENCE: OPD, Succeeding in School, p. 10
   OBJECTIVE: Take notes or write a summary or an outline
   STANDARD: CASAS 7.4.2
   OPD TERM: take notes

4. **ANSWER:** D
   REFERENCE: OPD, Succeeding in School, p. 10
   OBJECTIVE: Identify or use appropriate classroom behavior
   STANDARD: CASAS 0.1.5
   OPD TERM: check your work

5. **ANSWER:** B
   REFERENCE: OPD, Succeeding in School, p. 10
   OBJECTIVE: Identify or use appropriate language for informational purposes (e.g., to identify, describe, ask for information, state needs, command, agree or disagree, ask permission)
   STANDARD: CASAS 0.1.2
   OPD TERM: score

6. **ANSWER:** B
   REFERENCE: OPD, Succeeding in School, p. 10
   OBJECTIVE: Identify or use appropriate classroom behavior
   STANDARD: CASAS 0.1.5
   OPD TERM: answer sheet

7. **ANSWER:** A
   REFERENCE: OPD, Succeeding in School, p. 10
   OBJECTIVE: Identify or use appropriate classroom behavior
   STANDARD: CASAS 0.1.5
   OPD TERM: correct the mistake

8. **ANSWER:** D
   REFERENCE: OPD, Succeeding in School, p. 10
   OBJECTIVE: Identify or use appropriate classroom behavior
   STANDARD: CASAS 0.1.5
   OPD TERM: test booklet

9. **ANSWER:** C
   REFERENCE: OPD, Succeeding in School, p. 10
   OBJECTIVE: Identify or use appropriate classroom behavior
   STANDARD: CASAS 0.1.5
   OPD TERM: ask for help

10. **ANSWER:** A
    REFERENCE: OPD, Succeeding in School, p. 10
    OBJECTIVE: Identify or use appropriate classroom behavior
    STANDARD: CASAS 0.1.5
    OPD TERM: hand in your test

The Telephone, pp. 7–8

1. **ANSWER:** T
   REFERENCE: OPD, The Telephone, pp. 14–15
   OBJECTIVE: Use the telephone to make and receive routine personal and business calls
   STANDARD: CASAS 2.1.8
   OPD TERM: key pad

2. **ANSWER:** F
   REFERENCE: OPD, The Telephone, pp. 14–15
   OBJECTIVE: Use the telephone to make and receive routine personal and business calls
   STANDARD: CASAS 2.1.8
   OPD TERM: calling card

3. **ANSWER:** T
   REFERENCE: OPD, The Telephone, pp. 14–15
   OBJECTIVE: Use the telephone to make and receive routine personal and business calls
   STANDARD: CASAS 2.1.8
   OPD TERM: pound key

4. **ANSWER:** F
   REFERENCE: OPD, The Telephone, pp. 14–15
   OBJECTIVE: Use the telephone to make and receive routine personal and business calls
   STANDARD: CASAS 2.1.8
   OPD TERM: star key

5. **ANSWER:** T
   REFERENCE: OPD, The Telephone, pp. 14–15
   OBJECTIVE: Identify emergency numbers and place emergency calls
   STANDARD: CASAS 2.1.2
   OPD TERM: dial 911

6. **ANSWER:** T
   REFERENCE: OPD, The Telephone, pp. 14–15
   OBJECTIVE: Use the telephone to make and receive routine personal and business calls
   STANDARD: CASAS 2.1.8
   OPD TERM: charger

7. **ANSWER:** F
   REFERENCE: OPD, The Telephone, pp. 14–15
   OBJECTIVE: Take and interpret telephone messages, leave messages on answering machines, and interpret recorded messages
   STANDARD: CASAS 2.1.7
   OPD TERM: answering machine

8. **ANSWER:** D
   REFERENCE: OPD, The Telephone, pp. 14–15
   OBJECTIVE: Use the telephone to make and receive routine personal and business calls
   STANDARD: CASAS 2.1.8
   OPD TERM: press "send"

9. **ANSWER:** A
   REFERENCE: OPD, The Telephone, pp. 14–15
   OBJECTIVE: Use the telephone to make and receive routine personal and business calls
   STANDARD: CASAS 2.1.8
   OPD TERM: dial the phone number

10. **ANSWER:** B
    REFERENCE: OPD, The Telephone, pp. 14–15
    OBJECTIVE: Interpret information about time zones
    STANDARD: CASAS 2.1.3
    OPD TERM: international call

11. **ANSWER:** D
    REFERENCE: OPD, The Telephone, pp. 14–15
    OBJECTIVE: Interpret information about time zones
    STANDARD: CASAS 2.1.3
    OPD TERM: long distance call

12. **ANSWER:** A
    REFERENCE: OPD, The Telephone, pp. 14–15
    OBJECTIVE: Use the telephone to make and receive routine personal and business calls
    STANDARD: CASAS 2.1.8
    OPD TERM: local call

13. **ANSWER:** A
    REFERENCE: OPD, The Telephone, pp. 14–15
    OBJECTIVE: Use the telephone to make and receive routine personal and business calls
    STANDARD: CASAS 2.1.8
    OPD TERM: text message

14. **ANSWER:** D
    REFERENCE: OPD, The Telephone, pp. 14–15
    OBJECTIVE: Make comparisons, differentiating among, sorting, and classifying items, information, or ideas
    STANDARD: CASAS 7.2.3
    OPD TERM: voice message

15. **ANSWER:** C
    REFERENCE: OPD, The Telephone, pp. 14–15
    OBJECTIVE: Use the telephone to make and receive routine personal and business calls
    STANDARD: CASAS 2.1.8
    OPD TERM: receiver

The Calendar, pp. 9–10

1. **ANSWER:** F
   REFERENCE: OPD, The Calendar, pp. 20–21
   OBJECTIVE: Identify the months of the year and the days of the week
   STANDARD: CASAS 2.3.2
   OPD TERM: Monday

2. **ANSWER:** T
   REFERENCE: OPD, The Calendar, pp. 20–21
   OBJECTIVE: Identify the months of the year and the days of the week
   STANDARD: CASAS 2.3.2
   OPD TERM: date

3. **ANSWER:** F
   REFERENCE: OPD, The Calendar, pp. 20–21
   OBJECTIVE: Identify the months of the year and the days of the week
   STANDARD: CASAS 2.3.2
   OPD TERM: July

4. **ANSWER:** F
   REFERENCE: OPD, The Calendar, pp. 20–21
   OBJECTIVE: Identify the months of the year and the days of the week
   STANDARD: CASAS 2.3.2
   OPD TERM: May

5. **ANSWER:** A
   REFERENCE: OPD, The Calendar, pp. 20–21
   OBJECTIVE: Identify the months of the year and the days of the week
   STANDARD: CASAS 2.3.2
   OPD TERM: tomorrow

6. **ANSWER:** C
   REFERENCE: OPD, The Calendar, pp. 20–21
   OBJECTIVE: Identify the months of the year and the days of the week
   STANDARD: CASAS 2.3.2
   OPD TERM: Thursday

7. **ANSWER:** D
   REFERENCE: OPD, The Calendar, pp. 20–21
   OBJECTIVE: Identify the months of the year and the days of the week
   STANDARD: CASAS 2.3.2
   OPD TERM: yesterday

8. **ANSWER:** B
   REFERENCE: OPD, The Calendar, pp. 20–21
   OBJECTIVE: Identify the months of the year and the days of the week
   STANDARD: CASAS 2.3.2
   OPD TERM: month

9. **ANSWER:** D
   REFERENCE: OPD, The Calendar, pp. 20–21
   OBJECTIVE: Identify the months of the year and the days of the week
   STANDARD: CASAS 2.3.2
   OPD TERM: day

10. **ANSWER:** B
    REFERENCE: OPD, The Calendar, pp. 20–21
    OBJECTIVE: Identify the months of the year and the days of the week
    STANDARD: CASAS 2.3.2
    OPD TERM: today

11. **ANSWER:** B
    REFERENCE: OPD, The Calendar, pp. 20–21
    OBJECTIVE: Identify the months of the year and the days of the week
    STANDARD: CASAS 2.3.2
    OPD TERM: January

12. **ANSWER:** C
    REFERENCE: OPD, The Calendar, pp. 20–21
    OBJECTIVE: Identify the months of the year and the days of the week
    STANDARD: CASAS 2.3.2
    OPD TERM: March

13. **ANSWER:** A
    REFERENCE: OPD, The Calendar, pp. 20–21
    OBJECTIVE: Identify the months of the year and the days of the week
    STANDARD: CASAS 2.3.2
    OPD TERM: October

14. **ANSWER:** year
    REFERENCE: OPD, The Calendar, pp. 20–21
    OBJECTIVE: Identify the months of the year and the days of the week
    STANDARD: CASAS 2.3.2
    OPD TERM: year

15. **ANSWER:** Sunday
    REFERENCE: OPD, The Calendar, pp. 20–21
    OBJECTIVE: Identify the months of the year and the days of the week
    STANDARD: CASAS 2.3.2
    OPD TERM: Sunday

Calendar Events, pp. 11–12

1. **ANSWER:** T
   REFERENCE: OPD, Calendar Events, p. 22
   OBJECTIVE: Interpret information about holidays
   STANDARD: CASAS 2.7.1
   OPD TERM: wedding

2. **ANSWER:** T
   REFERENCE: OPD, Calendar Events, p. 22
   OBJECTIVE: Establish, maintain, and utilize a physical system of organization, such as notebooks, files, calendars, folders, and checklists
   STANDARD: CASAS 7.1.4
   OPD TERM: appointment

3. **ANSWER:** F
   REFERENCE: OPD, Calendar Events, p. 22
   OBJECTIVE: Interpret information about holidays
   STANDARD: CASAS 2.7.1
   OPD TERM: New Year's Day

4. **ANSWER:** F
   REFERENCE: OPD, Calendar Events, p. 22
   OBJECTIVE: Interpret information about holidays
   STANDARD: CASAS 2.7.1
   OPD TERM: Veterans Day

5. **ANSWER:** F
   REFERENCE: OPD, Calendar Events, p. 22
   OBJECTIVE: Interpret information about holidays
   STANDARD: CASAS 2.7.1
   OPD TERM: birthday

6. **ANSWER:** F
   REFERENCE: OPD, Calendar Events, p. 22
   OBJECTIVE: Interpret information about holidays
   STANDARD: CASAS 2.7.1
   OPD TERM: Thanksgiving

7. **ANSWER:** T
   REFERENCE: OPD, Calendar Events, p. 22
   OBJECTIVE: Interpret information about holidays
   STANDARD: CASAS 2.7.1
   OPD TERM: Presidents' Day

8. **ANSWER:** D
   REFERENCE: OPD, Calendar Events, p. 22
   OBJECTIVE: Interpret information about holidays
   STANDARD: CASAS 2.7.1
   OPD TERM: Memorial Day

9. **ANSWER:** C
   REFERENCE: OPD, Calendar Events, p. 22
   OBJECTIVE: Interpret information about holidays
   STANDARD: CASAS 2.7.1
   OPD TERM: Martin Luther King Jr. Day

10. **ANSWER:** C
    REFERENCE: OPD, Calendar Events, p. 22
    OBJECTIVE: Interpret information about holidays
    STANDARD: CASAS 2.7.1
    OPD TERM: religious holiday

11. **ANSWER:** A
    REFERENCE: OPD, Calendar Events, p. 22
    OBJECTIVE: Interpret information about holidays
    STANDARD: CASAS 2.7.1
    OPD TERM: Labor Day

12. **ANSWER:** Christmas
    REFERENCE: OPD, Calendar Events, p. 22
    OBJECTIVE: Interpret information about holidays
    STANDARD: CASAS 2.7.1
    OPD TERM: Christmas

13. **ANSWER:** legal
    REFERENCE: OPD, Calendar Events, p. 22
    OBJECTIVE: Interpret information about holidays
    STANDARD: CASAS 2.7.1
    OPD TERM: legal holiday

14. **ANSWER:** October
    REFERENCE: OPD, Calendar Events, p. 22
    OBJECTIVE: Interpret information about holidays
    STANDARD: CASAS 2.7.1
    OPD TERM: Columbus Day

15. **ANSWER:** Fourth of July
    REFERENCE: OPD, Calendar Events, p. 22
    OBJECTIVE: Interpret information about holidays
    STANDARD: CASAS 2.7.1
    OPD TERM: Fourth of July

Money, pp. 13–14

1. **ANSWER:** T
   REFERENCE: OPD, Money, p. 26
   OBJECTIVE: Count, convert, and use coins and currency, and recognize symbols such as ($) and (.)
   STANDARD: CASAS 1.1.6
   OPD TERM: a dime

2. **ANSWER:** F
   REFERENCE: OPD, Money, p. 26
   OBJECTIVE: Count, convert, and use coins and currency, and recognize symbols such as ($) and (.)
   STANDARD: CASAS 1.1.6
   OPD TERM: ten dollars

3. **ANSWER:** F
   REFERENCE: OPD, Money, p. 26
   OBJECTIVE: Count, convert, and use coins and currency, and recognize symbols such as ($) and (.)
   STANDARD: CASAS 1.1.6
   OPD TERM: five dollars

4. **ANSWER:** A
   REFERENCE: OPD, Money, p. 26
   OBJECTIVE: Count, convert, and use coins and currency, and recognize symbols such as ($) and (.)
   STANDARD: CASAS 1.1.6
   OPD TERM: a penny

5. **ANSWER:** B
   REFERENCE: OPD, Money, p. 26
   OBJECTIVE: Count, convert, and use coins and currency, and recognize symbols such as ($) and (.)
   STANDARD: CASAS 1.1.6
   OPD TERM: a quarter

6. **ANSWER:** A
   REFERENCE: OPD, Money, p. 26
   OBJECTIVE: Count, convert, and use coins and currency, and recognize symbols such as ($) and (.)
   STANDARD: CASAS 1.1.6
   OPD TERM: a dollar

7. **ANSWER:** D
   REFERENCE: OPD, Money, p. 26
   OBJECTIVE: Count, convert, and use coins and currency, and recognize symbols such as ($) and (.)
   STANDARD: CASAS 1.1.6
   OPD TERM: one hundred dollars

8. **ANSWER:** C
   REFERENCE: OPD, Money, p. 26
   OBJECTIVE: Count, convert, and use coins and currency, and recognize symbols such as ($) and (.)
   STANDARD: CASAS 1.1.6
   OPD TERM: borrow money

9. **ANSWER:** C
   REFERENCE: OPD, Money, p. 26
   OBJECTIVE: Count, convert, and use coins and currency, and recognize symbols such as ($) and (.)
   STANDARD: CASAS 1.1.6
   OPD TERM lend money

10. **ANSWER:** nickel
    REFERENCE: OPD, Money, p. 26
    OBJECTIVE: Count, convert, and use coins and currency, and recognize symbols such as ($) and (.)
    STANDARD: CASAS 1.1.6
    OPD TERM: a nickel

Shopping, pp. 15–16

1. **ANSWER:** T
   REFERENCE: OPD, Shopping, p. 27
   OBJECTIVE: Compare different methods used to purchase goods and services
   STANDARD: CASAS 1.3.1
   OPD TERM: buy

2. **ANSWER:** F
   REFERENCE: OPD, Shopping, p. 27
   OBJECTIVE: Identify or use various methods to purchase goods and services, and make returns and exchanges
   STANDARD: CASAS 1.3.3
   OPD TERM: return

3. **ANSWER:** F
   REFERENCE: OPD, Shopping, p. 27
   OBJECTIVE: Identify or use various methods to purchase goods and services, and make returns and exchanges
   STANDARD: CASAS 1.3.3
   OPD TERM: use a gift card

4. **ANSWER:** F
   REFERENCE: OPD, Shopping, p. 27
   OBJECTIVE: Identify or use various methods to purchase goods and services, and make returns and exchanges
   STANDARD: CASAS 1.3.3
   OPD TERM: use a credit card

5. **ANSWER:** A
   REFERENCE: OPD, Shopping, p. 27
   OBJECTIVE: Compare different methods used to purchase goods and services
   STANDARD: CASAS 1.3.1
   OPD TERM: pay cash

6. **ANSWER:** C
   REFERENCE: OPD, Shopping, p. 27
   OBJECTIVE: Interpret the procedures and forms associated with banking services, including writing checks
   STANDARD: CASAS 1.8.2
   OPD TERM: write a (personal) check

7. **ANSWER:** C
   REFERENCE: OPD, Shopping, p. 27
   OBJECTIVE Compare different methods used to purchase goods and services
   STANDARD: CASAS 1.3.1
   OPD TERM: receipt

8. **ANSWER:** D
   REFERENCE: OPD, Shopping, p. 27
   OBJECTIVE: Identify or use various methods to purchase goods and services, and make returns and exchanges
   STANDARD: CASAS 1.3.3
   OPD TERM: exchange

9. **ANSWER:** A
   REFERENCE: OPD, Shopping, p. 27
   OBJECTIVE: Demonstrate the use of savings and checking accounts, including using an ATM
   STANDARD: CASAS 1.8.1
   OPD TERM: use a debit card

10. **ANSWER:** D
    REFERENCE: OPD, Shopping, p. 27
    OBJECTIVE: Compare different methods used to purchase goods and services
    STANDARD: CASAS 1.3.1
    OPD TERM: cost

Describing People, pp. 17–18

1. **ANSWER:** F
   REFERENCE: OPD, Describing People, p. 32
   OBJECTIVE: Evaluate a situation, statement, or process, assembling information and providing evidence, making judgments, examining assumptions, and identifying contradictions
   STANDARD: CASAS 7.2.5
   OPD TERM: elderly

2. **ANSWER:** F
   REFERENCE: OPD, Describing People, p. 32
   OBJECTIVE: Evaluate a situation, statement, or process, assembling information and providing evidence, making judgments, examining assumptions, and identifying contradictions
   STANDARD: CASAS 7.2.5
   OPD TERM: short

3. **ANSWER:** A
   REFERENCE: OPD, Describing People, p. 32
   OBJECTIVE: Evaluate a situation, statement, or process, assembling information and providing evidence, making judgments, examining assumptions, and identifying contradictions
   STANDARD: CASAS 7.2.5
   OPD TERM: cute

4. **ANSWER:** D
   REFERENCE: OPD, Describing People, p. 32
   OBJECTIVE: Evaluate a situation, statement, or process, assembling information and providing evidence, making judgments, examining assumptions, and identifying contradictions
   STANDARD: CASAS 7.2.5
   OPD TERM: young

5. **ANSWER:** A
   REFERENCE: OPD, Describing People, p. 32
   OBJECTIVE: Evaluate a situation, statement, or process, assembling information and providing evidence, making judgments, examining assumptions, and identifying contradictions
   STANDARD: CASAS 7.2.5
   OPD TERM: thin

6. **ANSWER:** B
   REFERENCE: OPD, Describing People, p. 32
   OBJECTIVE: Evaluate a situation, statement, or process, assembling information and providing evidence, making judgments, examining assumptions, and identifying contradictions
   STANDARD: CASAS 7.2.5
   OPD TERM: heavy

7. **ANSWER:** B
   REFERENCE: OPD, Describing People, p. 32
   OBJECTIVE: Evaluate a situation, statement, or process, assembling information and providing evidence, making judgments, examining assumptions, and identifying contradictions
   STANDARD: CASAS 7.2.5
   OPD TERM: middle-aged

8. **ANSWER:** D
   REFERENCE: OPD, Describing People, p. 32
   OBJECTIVE: Evaluate a situation, statement, or process, assembling information and providing evidence, making judgments, examining assumptions, and identifying contradictions
   STANDARD: CASAS 7.2.5
   OPD TERM: pregnant

9. **ANSWER:** B
   REFERENCE: OPD, Describing People, p. 32
   OBJECTIVE: Evaluate a situation, statement, or process, assembling information and providing evidence, making judgments, examining assumptions, and identifying contradictions
   STANDARD: CASAS 7.2.5
   OPD TERM: tall

10. **ANSWER:** A
    REFERENCE: OPD, Describing People, p. 32
    OBJECTIVE: Evaluate a situation, statement, or process, assembling information and providing evidence, making judgments, examining assumptions, and identifying contradictions
    STANDARD: CASAS 7.2.5
    OPD TERM: attractive

Childcare and Parenting, pp. 19–20

1. **ANSWER:** T
   REFERENCE: OPD, Childcare and Parenting, pp. 36–37
   OBJECTIVE: Evaluate a situation, statement, or process, assembling information and providing evidence, making judgments, examining assumptions, and identifying contradictions
   STANDARD: CASAS 7.2.5
   OPD TERM: baby bag

2. **ANSWER:** F
   REFERENCE: OPD, Childcare and Parenting, pp. 36–37
   OBJECTIVE: Evaluate a situation, statement, or process, assembling information and providing evidence, making judgments, examining assumptions, and identifying contradictions
   STANDARD: CASAS 7.2.5
   OPD TERM: kiss goodnight

3. **ANSWER:** B
   REFERENCE: OPD, Childcare and Parenting, pp. 36–37
   OBJECTIVE: Identify or make inferences through inductive and deductive reasoning to hypothesize, predict, conclude, and synthesize; distinguish fact from opinion, and determine what is mandatory and what is discretionary
   STANDARD: CASAS 7.2.4
   OPD TERM: sing a lullaby

4. **ANSWER:** C
   REFERENCE: OPD, Childcare and Parenting, pp. 36–37
   OBJECTIVE: Identify child-rearing practices and community resources that assist in developing parenting skills
   STANDARD: CASAS 3.5.7
   OPD TERM: stroller

5. **ANSWER:** D
   REFERENCE: OPD, Childcare and Parenting, pp. 36–37
   OBJECTIVE: Identify child-rearing practices and community resources that assist in developing parenting skills
   STANDARD: CASAS 3.5.7
   OPD TERM: feed

6. **ANSWER:** A
   REFERENCE: OPD, Childcare and Parenting, pp. 36–37
   OBJECTIVE: Identify child-rearing practices and community resources that assist in developing parenting skills
   STANDARD: CASAS 3.5.7
   OPD TERM: read to

7. **ANSWER:** A
   REFERENCE: OPD, Childcare and Parenting, pp. 36–37
   OBJECTIVE: Devise and implement a solution to an identified problem
   STANDARD: CASAS 7.3.2
   OPD TERM: change a diaper

8. **ANSWER:** B
   REFERENCE: OPD, Childcare and Parenting, pp. 36–37
   OBJECTIVE: Converse about daily and leisure activities and personal interests
   STANDARD: CASAS 0.2.4
   OPD TERM: play with

9. **ANSWER:** A
   REFERENCE: OPD, Childcare and Parenting, pp. 36–37
   OBJECTIVE: Identify child-rearing practices and community resources that assist in developing parenting skills
   STANDARD: CASAS 3.5.7
   OPD TERM: hold

10. **ANSWER:** bathe
    REFERENCE: OPD, Childcare and Parenting, pp. 36–37
    OBJECTIVE: Identify child-rearing practices and community resources that assist in developing parenting skills
    STANDARD: CASAS 3.5.7
    OPD TERM: bathe

Daily Routines, pp. 21–22

1. **ANSWER:** F
   REFERENCE: OPD, Daily Routines, pp. 38–39
   OBJECTIVE: Evaluate a situation, statement, or process, assembling information and providing evidence, making judgments, examining assumptions, and identifying contradictions
   STANDARD: CASAS 7.2.5
   OPD TERM: have dinner

2. **ANSWER:** T
   REFERENCE: OPD, Daily Routines, pp. 38–39
   OBJECTIVE: Evaluate a situation, statement, or process, assembling information and providing evidence, making judgments, examining assumptions, and identifying contradictions
   STANDARD: CASAS 7.2.5
   OPD TERM: cook dinner

3. **ANSWER:** A
   REFERENCE: OPD, Daily Routines, pp. 38–39
   OBJECTIVE: Demonstrate an organized approach to achieving goals, including identifying and prioritizing tasks and setting and following an effective schedule
   STANDARD: CASAS 7.1.2
   OPD TERM: get up

4. **ANSWER:** C
   REFERENCE: OPD, Daily Routines, pp. 38–39
   OBJECTIVE: Identify or use appropriate language for informational purposes
   STANDARD: CASAS 0.1.2
   OPD TERM: go to bed

5. **ANSWER:** B
   REFERENCE: OPD, Daily Routines, pp. 38–39
   OBJECTIVE: Converse about daily and leisure activities and personal interests
   STANDARD: CASAS 0.2.4
   OPD TERM: work

6. **ANSWER:** D
   REFERENCE: OPD, Daily Routines, pp. 38–39
   OBJECTIVE: Converse about daily and leisure activities and personal interests
   STANDARD: CASAS 0.2.4
   OPD TERM: take a shower

7. **ANSWER:** B
   REFERENCE: OPD, Daily Routines, pp. 38–39
   OBJECTIVE: Identify practices that promote physical well-being
   STANDARD: CASAS 3.5.9
   OPD TERM: exercise

8. **ANSWER:** C
   REFERENCE: OPD, Daily Routines, pp. 38–39
   OBJECTIVE: Converse about daily and leisure activities and personal interests
   STANDARD: CASAS 0.2.4
   OPD TERM: make lunch

9. **ANSWER:** A
   REFERENCE: OPD, Daily Routines, pp. 38–39
   OBJECTIVE: Interpret diagrams, illustrations, and scale drawings
   STANDARD: CASAS 6.6.5
   OPD TERM: drive to work

10. **ANSWER:** A
    REFERENCE: OPD, Daily Routines, pp. 38–39
    OBJECTIVE: Recognize and/or demonstrate housekeeping and house cleaning tasks
    STANDARD: CASAS 8.2.3
    OPD TERM: clean the house

The Home, pp. 23–24

1. **ANSWER:** T
   REFERENCE: OPD, The Home, pp. 46–47
   OBJECTIVE: Identify different kinds of housing, areas of the home, and common household items
   STANDARD: CASAS 1.4.1
   OPD TERM: door

2. **ANSWER:** F
   REFERENCE: OPD, The Home, pp. 46–47
   OBJECTIVE: Identify different kinds of housing, areas of the home, and common household items
   STANDARD: CASAS 1.4.1
   OPD TERM: basement

3. **ANSWER:** F
   REFERENCE: OPD, The Home, pp. 46–47
   OBJECTIVE: Identify different kinds of housing, areas of the home, and common household items
   STANDARD: CASAS 1.4.1
   OPD TERM: bathroom

4. **ANSWER:** C
   REFERENCE: OPD, The Home, pp. 46–47
   OBJECTIVE: Identify different kinds of housing, areas of the home, and common household items
   STANDARD: CASAS 1.4.1
   OPD TERM: bedroom

5. **ANSWER:** D
   REFERENCE: OPD, The Home, pp. 46–47
   OBJECTIVE: Identify different kinds of housing, areas of the home, and common household items
   STANDARD: CASAS 1.4.1
   OPD TERM: kitchen

6. **ANSWER:** A
   REFERENCE OPD, The Home, pp. 46–47
   OBJECTIVE: Make comparisons, differentiating among, sorting, and classifying items, information, or ideas
   STANDARD: CASAS 7.2.3
   OPD TERM: window

7. **ANSWER:** B
   REFERENCE: OPD, The Home, pp. 46–47
   OBJECTIVE: Identify different kinds of housing, areas of the home, and common household items
   STANDARD: CASAS 1.4.1
   OPD TERM: living room

8. **ANSWER:** D
   REFERENCE: OPD, The Home, pp. 46–47
   OBJECTIVE: Identify different kinds of housing, areas of the home, and common household items
   STANDARD: CASAS 1.4.1
   OPD TERM: floor

9. **ANSWER:** C
   REFERENCE: OPD, The Home, pp. 46–47
   OBJECTIVE: Identify different kinds of housing, areas of the home, and common household items
   STANDARD: CASAS 1.4.1
   OPD TERM: dining area

10. **ANSWER:** D
    REFERENCE: OPD, The Home, pp. 46–47
    OBJECTIVE: Identify different kinds of housing, areas of the home, and common household items
    STANDARD: CASAS 1.4.1
    OPD TERM: garage

Finding a Home, pp. 25–26

1. **ANSWER:** T
   REFERENCE: OPD, Finding a Home, pp. 48–49
   OBJECTIVE: Interpret information about housing loans and home-related insurance
   STANDARD: CASAS 1.4.6
   OPD TERM: get a loan

2. **ANSWER:** F
   REFERENCE: OPD, Finding a Home, pp. 48–49
   OBJECTIVE: Evaluate a situation, statement, or process, assembling information and providing evidence, making judgments, examining assumptions, and identifying contradictions
   STANDARD: CASAS 7.2.5
   OPD TERM: take ownership

3. **ANSWER:** A
   REFERENCE: OPD, Finding a Home, pp. 48–49
   OBJECTIVE: Identify or make inferences through inductive and deductive reasoning to hypothesize, predict, conclude, and synthesize; distinguish fact from opinion, and determine what is mandatory and what is discretionary
   STANDARD: CASAS 7.2.4
   OPD TERM: unpack

4. **ANSWER:** B
   REFERENCE: OPD, Finding a Home, pp. 48–49
   OBJECTIVE: Interpret information about housing loans and home-related insurance
   STANDARD: CASAS 1.4.6
   OPD TERM: make a mortgage payment

5. **ANSWER:** B
   REFERENCE: OPD, Finding a Home, pp. 48–49
   OBJECTIVE: Select appropriate housing by interpreting classified ads, signs, and other information
   STANDARD: CASAS 1.4.2
   OPD TERM: meet with a realtor

6. **ANSWER:** D
   REFERENCE: OPD, Finding a Home, pp. 48–49
   OBJECTIVE: Interpret lease and rental agreements
   STANDARD: CASAS 1.4.3
   OPD TERM: call the manager

7. **ANSWER:** B
   REFERENCE: OPD, Finding a Home, pp. 48–49
   OBJECTIVE: Select appropriate housing by interpreting classified ads, signs, and other information
   STANDARD: CASAS 1.4.2
   OPD TERM: look at houses

8. **ANSWER:** C
   REFERENCE: OPD, Finding a Home, pp. 48–49
   OBJECTIVE: Select appropriate housing by interpreting classified ads, signs, and other information
   STANDARD: CASAS 1.4.2
   OPD TERM: Internet listing

9. **ANSWER:** A
   REFERENCE: OPD, Finding a Home, pp. 48–49
   OBJECTIVE: Interpret lease and rental agreements
   STANDARD: CASAS 1.4.3
   OPD TERM: meet the neighbors

10. **ANSWER:** furnished apartment
    REFERENCE: OPD, Finding a Home, pp. 48–49
    OBJECTIVE: Identify different kinds of housing, areas of the home, and common household items
    STANDARD: CASAS 1.4.1
    OPD TERM: furnished apartment

11. **ANSWER:** utilities
    REFERENCE: OPD, Finding a Home, pp. 48–49
    OBJECTIVE: Identify or use appropriate language for informational purposes
    STANDARD: CASAS 0.1.2
    OPD TERM: utilities

12. **ANSWER:** classified ads
    REFERENCE: OPD, Finding a Home, pp. 48–49
    OBJECTIVE: Select appropriate housing by interpreting classified ads, signs, and other information
    STANDARD: CASAS 1.4.2
    OPD TERM: classified ad

13. **ANSWER:** pack
    REFERENCE: OPD, Finding a Home, pp. 48–49
    OBJECTIVE: Identify or use appropriate language for informational purposes
    STANDARD: CASAS 0.1.2
    OPD TERM: pack

14. **ANSWER:** paint
    REFERENCE: OPD, Finding a Home, pp. 48–49
    OBJECTIVE: Identify or use appropriate language for informational purposes
    STANDARD: CASAS 0.1.2
    OPD TERM: paint

15. **ANSWER:** rental agreement
    REFERENCE: OPD, Finding a Home, pp. 48–49
    OBJECTIVE: Interpret lease and rental agreements
    STANDARD: CASAS 1.4.3
    OPD TERM: sign the rental agreement

Different Places to Live, pp. 27–28

1. **ANSWER:** F
   REFERENCE: OPD, Different Places to Live, p. 52
   OBJECTIVE: Evaluate a situation, statement, or process, assembling information and providing evidence, making judgments, examining assumptions, and identifying contradictions
   STANDARD: CASAS 7.2.5
   OPD TERM: the suburbs

2. **ANSWER:** F
   REFERENCE: OPD, Different Places to Live, p. 52
   OBJECTIVE: Identify different kinds of housing, areas of the home, and common household items
   STANDARD: CASAS 1.4.1
   OPD TERM: townhouse

3. **ANSWER:** T
   REFERENCE: OPD, Different Places to Live, p. 52
   OBJECTIVE: Evaluate a situation, statement, or process, assembling information and providing evidence, making judgments, examining assumptions, and identifying contradictions
   STANDARD: CASAS 7.2.5
   OPD TERM: the country

4. **ANSWER:** D
   REFERENCE: OPD, Different Places to Live, p. 52
   OBJECTIVE: Identify different kinds of housing, areas of the home, and common household items
   STANDARD: CASAS 1.4.1
   OPD TERM: college dormitory

5. **ANSWER:** C
   REFERENCE: OPD, Different Places to Live, p. 52
   OBJECTIVE: Make comparisons, differentiating among, sorting, and classifying items, information, or ideas
   STANDARD: CASAS 7.2.3
   OPD TERM: nursing home

6. **ANSWER:** B
   REFERENCE: OPD, Different Places to Live, p. 52
   OBJECTIVE: Identify different kinds of housing, areas of the home, and common household items
   STANDARD: CASAS 1.4.1
   OPD TERM: farm

7. ANSWER: A
REFERENCE: OPD, Different Places to Live, p. 52
OBJECTIVE: Identify or make inferences through inductive and deductive reasoning to hypothesize, predict, conclude, and synthesize; distinguish fact from opinion, and determine what is mandatory and what is discretionary
STANDARD: CASAS 7.2.4
OPD TERM: the city

8. ANSWER: D
REFERENCE: OPD, Different Places to Live, p. 52
OBJECTIVE: Identify different kinds of housing, areas of the home, and common household items
STANDARD: CASAS 1.4.1
OPD TERM: mobile home

9. ANSWER: B
REFERENCE: OPD, Different Places to Live, p. 52
OBJECTIVE: Identify or make inferences through inductive and deductive reasoning to hypothesize, predict, conclude, and synthesize; distinguish fact from opinion, and determine what is mandatory and what is discretionary
STANDARD: CASAS 7.2.4
OPD TERM: a small town

10. ANSWER: A
REFERENCE: OPD, Different Places to Live, p. 52
OBJECTIVE: Identify different kinds of housing, areas of the home, and common household items
STANDARD: CASAS 1.4.1
OPD TERM: condominium

Household Problems and Repairs, pp. 29–30

1. ANSWER: T
REFERENCE: OPD, Household Problems and Repairs, pp. 62–63
OBJECTIVE: Interpret information about home maintenance, and communicate housing problems to a landlord
STANDARD: CASAS 1.4.7
OPD TERM: the roof is leaking

2. ANSWER: T
REFERENCE: OPD, Household Problems and Repairs, pp. 62–63
OBJECTIVE: Identify common occupations and the skills and education required for them
STANDARD: CASAS 4.1.8
OPD TERM: locksmith

3. ANSWER: A
REFERENCE: OPD, Household Problems and Repairs, pp. 62–63
OBJECTIVE: Identify common tools, equipment, machines, and materials required for one's job
STANDARD: CASAS 4.5.1
OPD TERM: plumber

4. ANSWER: D
REFERENCE: OPD, Household Problems and Repairs, pp. 62–63
OBJECTIVE: Identify common occupations and the skills and education required for them
STANDARD: CASAS 4.1.8
OPD TERM: exterminator

5. ANSWER: B
REFERENCE: OPD, Household Problems and Repairs, pp. 62–63
OBJECTIVE: Identify or make inferences through inductive and deductive reasoning to hypothesize, predict, conclude, and synthesize; distinguish fact from opinion, and determine what is mandatory and what is discretionary
STANDARD: CASAS 7.2.4
OPD TERM: termites

6. ANSWER: B
REFERENCE: OPD, Household Problems and Repairs, pp. 62–63
OBJECTIVE: Identify or make inferences through inductive and deductive reasoning to hypothesize, predict, conclude, and synthesize; distinguish fact from opinion, and determine what is mandatory and what is discretionary
STANDARD: CASAS 7.2.4
OPD TERM: the power is out

7. ANSWER: D
REFERENCE: OPD, Household Problems and Repairs, pp. 62–63
OBJECTIVE: Recognize and/or demonstrate general household repair and maintenance
STANDARD: CASAS 8.2.6
OPD TERM: the sink is overflowing

8. ANSWER: A
REFERENCE: OPD, Household Problems and Repairs, pp. 62–63
OBJECTIVE: Identify common occupations and the skills and education required for them
STANDARD: CASAS 4.1.8
OPD TERM: electrician

9. ANSWER: broken
REFERENCE: OPD, Household Problems and Repairs, pp. 62–63
OBJECTIVE: Interpret information about home maintenance, and communicate housing problems to a landlord
STANDARD: CASAS 1.4.7
OPD TERM: the window is broken

10. ANSWER: roofer
REFERENCE: OPD, Household Problems and Repairs, pp. 62–63
OBJECTIVE: Identify common occupations and the skills and education required for them
STANDARD: CASAS 4.1.8
OPD TERM: roofer

A Grocery Store, pp. 31–32

1. ANSWER: T
REFERENCE: OPD, A Grocery Store, pp. 72–73
OBJECTIVE: Identify common occupations and the skills and education required for them
STANDARD: CASAS 4.1.8
OPD TERM: cashier

2. ANSWER: T
REFERENCE: OPD, A Grocery Store, pp. 72–73
OBJECTIVE: Identify or use various methods to purchase goods and services, and make returns and exchanges
STANDARD: CASAS 1.3.3
OPD TERM: cart

3. ANSWER: F
REFERENCE: OPD, A Grocery Store, pp. 72–73
OBJECTIVE: Identify common occupations and the skills and education required for them
STANDARD: CASAS 4.1.8
OPD TERM: manager

4. ANSWER: F
REFERENCE: OPD, A Grocery Store, pp. 72–73
OBJECTIVE: Identify common occupations and the skills and education required for them
STANDARD: CASAS 4.1.8
OPD TERM: bagger

5. ANSWER: F
REFERENCE: OPD, A Grocery Store, pp. 72–73
OBJECTIVE: Identify or use various methods to purchase goods and services, and make returns and exchanges
STANDARD: CASAS 1.3.3
OPD TERM: line

6. ANSWER: T
REFERENCE: OPD, A Grocery Store, pp. 72–73
OBJECTIVE: Identify or use various methods to purchase goods and services, and make returns and exchanges
STANDARD: CASAS 1.3.3
OPD TERM: aisle

7. ANSWER: D
REFERENCE: OPD, A Grocery Store, pp. 72–73
OBJECTIVE: Interpret information or directions to locate merchandise
STANDARD: CASAS 1.3.7
OPD TERM: tuna

8. ANSWER: C
REFERENCE: OPD, A Grocery Store, pp. 72–73
OBJECTIVE: Interpret information or directions to locate merchandise
STANDARD: CASAS 1.3.7
OPD TERM: yogurt

9. ANSWER: B
REFERENCE: OPD, A Grocery Store, pp. 72–73
OBJECTIVE: Recognize and/or demonstrate meal and snack preparation tasks and activities
STANDARD: CASAS 8.2.1
OPD TERM: oil

10. ANSWER: A
REFERENCE: OPD, A Grocery Store, pp. 72–73
OBJECTIVE: Make comparisons, differentiating among, sorting, and classifying items, information, or ideas
STANDARD: CASAS 7.2.3
OPD TERM: sugar

11. ANSWER: B
REFERENCE: OPD, A Grocery Store, pp. 72–73
OBJECTIVE: Interpret information or directions to locate merchandise
STANDARD: CASAS 1.3.7
OPD TERM: beans

12. ANSWER: D
REFERENCE: OPD, A Grocery Store, pp. 72–73
OBJECTIVE: Recognize and/or demonstrate meal and snack preparation tasks and activities
STANDARD: CASAS 8.2.1
OPD TERM: flour

13. ANSWER: B
REFERENCE: OPD, A Grocery Store, pp. 72–73
OBJECTIVE: Identify common food items
STANDARD: CASAS 1.3.8
OPD TERM: ice cream

14. ANSWER: cookies
REFERENCE: OPD, A Grocery Store, pp. 72–73
OBJECTIVE: Identify common food items
STANDARD: CASAS 1.3.8
OPD TERM: cookies

15. ANSWER: customer
REFERENCE: OPD, A Grocery Store, pp. 72–73
OBJECTIVE: Identify or use appropriate language for informational purposes; (e.g., to identify, describe, ask for information, state needs, command, agree or disagree, ask permission)
STANDARD: CASAS 0.1.2
OPD TERM: customer

Containers and Packaging, pp. 33–34

1. ANSWER: T
REFERENCE: OPD, Containers and Packaging, p. 74
OBJECTIVE: Identify product containers and interpret weight and volume
STANDARD: CASAS 1.1.7
OPD TERM: containers

2. **ANSWER:** F
   REFERENCE: OPD, Containers and Packaging, p. 74
   OBJECTIVE: Evaluate a situation, statement, or process, assembling information and providing evidence, making judgments, examining assumptions, and identifying contradictions
   STANDARD: CASAS 7.2.5
   OPD TERM: cans

3. **ANSWER:** D
   REFERENCE: OPD, Containers and Packaging, p. 74
   OBJECTIVE: Identify product containers and interpret weight and volume
   STANDARD: CASAS 1.1.7
   OPD TERM: six-packs

4. **ANSWER:** C
   REFERENCE: OPD, Containers and Packaging, p. 74
   OBJECTIVE: Identify product containers and interpret weight and volume
   STANDARD: CASAS 1.1.7
   OPD TERM: boxes

5. **ANSWER:** A
   REFERENCE: OPD, Containers and Packaging, p. 74
   OBJECTIVE: Identify product containers and interpret weight and volume
   STANDARD: CASAS 1.1.7
   OPD TERM: jars

6. **ANSWER:** B
   REFERENCE: OPD, Containers and Packaging, p. 74
   OBJECTIVE: Identify product containers and interpret weight and volume
   STANDARD: CASAS 1.1.7
   OPD TERM: a tube of toothpaste

7. **ANSWER:** A
   REFERENCE: OPD, Containers and Packaging, p. 74
   OBJECTIVE: Identify product containers and interpret weight and volume
   STANDARD: CASAS 1.1.7
   OPD TERM: a loaf of bread

8. **ANSWER:** C
   REFERENCE: OPD, Containers and Packaging, p. 74
   OBJECTIVE: Identify product containers and interpret weight and volume
   STANDARD: CASAS 1.1.7
   OPD TERM: bags

9. **ANSWER:** bottle
   REFERENCE: OPD, Containers and Packaging, p. 74
   OBJECTIVE: Identify product containers and interpret weight and volume
   STANDARD: CASAS 1.1.7
   OPD TERM: bottles

10. **ANSWER:** carton of eggs
    REFERENCE: OPD, Containers and Packaging, p. 74
    OBJECTIVE: Identify common food items
    STANDARD: CASAS 1.3.8
    OPD TERM: a carton of eggs

Weights and Measurements, pp. 35–36

1. **ANSWER:** T
   REFERENCE: OPD, Weights and Measurements, p. 75
   OBJECTIVE: Select, compute, or interpret appropriate standard measurement for length, width, perimeter, area, volume, height, or weight
   STANDARD: CASAS 1.1.4
   OPD TERM: weigh the food

2. **ANSWER:** T
   REFERENCE: OPD, Weights and Measurements, p. 75
   OBJECTIVE: Evaluate a situation, statement, or process, assembling information and providing evidence, making judgments, examining assumptions, and identifying contradictions
   STANDARD: CASAS 7.2.5
   OPD TERM: measure the ingredients

3. **ANSWER:** D
   REFERENCE: OPD, Weights and Measurements, p. 75
   OBJECTIVE: Identify product containers and interpret weight and volume
   STANDARD: CASAS 1.1.7
   OPD TERM: a gallon of water

4. **ANSWER:** A
   REFERENCE: OPD, Weights and Measurements, p. 75
   OBJECTIVE: Select, compute, or interpret appropriate standard measurement for length, width, perimeter, area, volume, height, or weight
   STANDARD: CASAS 1.1.4
   OPD TERM: an ounce of cheese

5. **ANSWER:** B
   REFERENCE: OPD, Weights and Measurements, p. 75
   OBJECTIVE: Identify product containers and interpret weight and volume
   STANDARD: CASAS 1.1.7
   OPD TERM: a pint of frozen yogurt

6. **ANSWER:** C
   REFERENCE: OPD, Weights and Measurements, p. 75
   OBJECTIVE: Select, compute, or interpret appropriate standard measurement for length, width, perimeter, area, volume, height, or weight
   STANDARD: CASAS 1.1.4
   OPD TERM: a tablespoon of sugar

7. **ANSWER:** B
   REFERENCE: OPD, Weights and Measurements, p. 75
   OBJECTIVE: Select, compute, or interpret appropriate standard measurement for length, width, perimeter, area, volume, height, or weight
   STANDARD: CASAS 1.1.4
   OPD TERM: a cup of oil

8. **ANSWER:** A
   REFERENCE: OPD, Weights and Measurements, p. 75
   OBJECTIVE: Select, compute, or interpret appropriate standard measurement for length, width, perimeter, area, volume, height, or weight
   STANDARD: CASAS 1.1.4
   OPD TERM: a teaspoon of salt

9. **ANSWER:** B
   REFERENCE: OPD, Weights and Measurements, p. 75
   OBJECTIVE: Select, compute, or interpret appropriate standard measurement for length, width, perimeter, area, volume, height, or weight
   STANDARD: CASAS 1.1.4
   OPD TERM: a pound of roast beef

10. **ANSWER:** C
    REFERENCE: OPD, Weights and Measurements, p. 75
    OBJECTIVE: Select, compute, or interpret appropriate standard measurement for length, width, perimeter, area, volume, height, or weight
    STANDARD: CASAS 1.1.4
    OPD TERM: a quarter cup of brown sugar

Food Preparation and Safety, pp. 37–38

1. **ANSWER:** F
   REFERENCE: OPD, Food Preparation and Safety, pp. 76–77
   OBJECTIVE: Recognize and/or demonstrate meal and snack preparation tasks and activities
   STANDARD: CASAS 8.2.1
   OPD TERM: scrambled eggs

2. **ANSWER:** T
   REFERENCE: OPD, Food Preparation and Safety, pp. 76–77
   OBJECTIVE: Recognize and/or demonstrate meal and snack preparation tasks and activities
   STANDARD: CASAS 8.2.1
   OPD TERM: boiled ham

3. **ANSWER:** B
   REFERENCE: OPD, Food Preparation and Safety, pp. 76–77
   OBJECTIVE: Recognize and/or demonstrate meal and snack preparation tasks and activities
   STANDARD: CASAS 8.2.1
   OPD TERM: roasted turkey

4. **ANSWER:** D
   REFERENCE: OPD, Food Preparation and Safety, pp. 76–77
   OBJECTIVE: Recognize and/or demonstrate meal and snack preparation tasks and activities
   STANDARD: CASAS 8.2.1
   OPD TERM: fried chicken

5. **ANSWER:** A
   REFERENCE: OPD, Food Preparation and Safety, pp. 76–77
   OBJECTIVE: Recognize and/or demonstrate meal and snack preparation tasks and activities
   STANDARD: CASAS 8.2.1
   OPD TERM: boil the chicken

6. **ANSWER:** B
   REFERENCE: OPD, Food Preparation and Safety, pp. 76–77
   OBJECTIVE: Recognize and/or demonstrate meal and snack preparation tasks and activities
   STANDARD: CASAS 8.2.1
   OPD TERM: bake

7. **ANSWER:** A
   REFERENCE: OPD, Food Preparation and Safety, pp. 76–77
   OBJECTIVE: Recognize and/or demonstrate meal and snack preparation tasks and activities
   STANDARD: CASAS 8.2.1
   OPD TERM: steam the broccoli

8. **ANSWER:** C
   REFERENCE: OPD, Food Preparation and Safety, pp. 76–77
   OBJECTIVE: Recognize and/or demonstrate meal and snack preparation tasks and activities
   STANDARD: CASAS 8.2.1
   OPD TERM: barbecued ribs

9. **ANSWER:** C
   REFERENCE: OPD, Food Preparation and Safety, pp. 76–77
   OBJECTIVE: Recognize and/or demonstrate meal and snack preparation tasks and activities
   STANDARD: CASAS 8.2.1
   OPD TERM: cut up the chicken

10. **ANSWER:** peel
    REFERENCE: OPD, Food Preparation and Safety, pp. 76–77
    OBJECTIVE: Recognize and/or demonstrate meal and snack preparation tasks and activities
    STANDARD: CASAS 8.2.1
    OPD TERM: peel the carrots

A Restaurant, pp. 39–40

1. **ANSWER:** F
   REFERENCE: OPD, A Restaurant, pp. 82–83
   OBJECTIVE: Identify common occupations and the skills and education required for them
   STANDARD: CASAS 4.1.8
   OPD TERM: busser

2. **ANSWER:** T
   REFERENCE: OPD, A Restaurant, pp. 82–83
   OBJECTIVE: Interpret and order from restaurant and fast food menus, and compute related costs
   STANDARD: CASAS 2.6.4
   OPD TERM: menu

3. **ANSWER:** B
   REFERENCE: OPD, A Restaurant, pp. 82–83
   OBJECTIVE: Recognize and/or demonstrate meal and snack preparation tasks and activities
   STANDARD: CASAS 8.2.1
   OPD TERM: set the table

4. **ANSWER:** B
   REFERENCE: OPD, A Restaurant, pp. 82–83
   OBJECTIVE: Converse about daily and leisure activities and personal interests
   STANDARD: CASAS 0.2.4
   OPD TERM: pay the check

5. **ANSWER:** C
   REFERENCE: OPD, A Restaurant, pp. 82–83
   OBJECTIVE: Recognize and/or demonstrate dining skills and manners
   STANDARD: CASAS 8.1.3
   OPD TERM: leave a tip

6. **ANSWER:** B
   REFERENCE: OPD, A Restaurant, pp. 82–83
   OBJECTIVE: Identify common occupations and the skills and education required for them
   STANDARD: CASAS 4.1.8
   OPD TERM: take the order

7. **ANSWER:** A
   REFERENCE: OPD, A Restaurant, pp. 82–83
   OBJECTIVE: Recognize and/or demonstrate meal and snack preparation tasks and activities
   STANDARD: CASAS 8.2.1
   OPD TERM: high chair

8. **ANSWER:** C
   REFERENCE: OPD, A Restaurant, pp. 82–83
   OBJECTIVE: Interpret and order from restaurant and fast food menus, and compute related costs
   STANDARD: CASAS 2.6.4
   OPD TERM: order from the menu

9. **ANSWER:** A
   REFERENCE: OPD, A Restaurant, pp. 82–83
   OBJECTIVE: Identify common occupations and the skills and education required for them
   STANDARD: CASAS 4.1.8
   OPD TERM: waiter

10. **ANSWER:** waitress
    REFERENCE: OPD, A Restaurant, pp. 82–83
    OBJECTIVE: Identify common occupations and the skills and education required for them
    STANDARD: CASAS 4.1.8
    OPD TERM: waitress

Workplace Clothing, pp. 41–42

1. **ANSWER:** T
   REFERENCE: OPD, Workplace Clothing, pp. 92–93
   OBJECTIVE: Identify common articles of clothing
   STANDARD: CASAS 1.3.9
   OPD TERM: work shirt

2. **ANSWER:** F
   REFERENCE: OPD, Workplace Clothing, pp. 92–93
   OBJECTIVE: Identify appropriate behavior, attire, attitudes, and social interaction, and other factors that affect job retention and advancement
   STANDARD: CASAS 4.4.1
   OPD TERM: lab coat

3. **ANSWER:** F
   REFERENCE: OPD, Workplace Clothing, pp. 92–93
   OBJECTIVE: Identify or make inferences through inductive and deductive reasoning to hypothesize, predict, conclude, and synthesize; distinguish fact from opinion, and determine what is mandatory and what is discretionary
   STANDARD: CASAS 7.2.4
   OPD TERM: apron

4. **ANSWER:** B
   REFERENCE: OPD, Workplace Clothing, pp. 92–93
   OBJECTIVE: Identify safe work procedures and common safety equipment, including wearing safe work attire
   STANDARD: CASAS 4.3.3
   OPD TERM: face mask

5. **ANSWER:** A
   REFERENCE: OPD, Workplace Clothing, pp. 92–93
   OBJECTIVE: Identify safe work procedures and common safety equipment, including wearing safe work attire
   STANDARD: CASAS 4.3.3
   OPD TERM: hard hat

6. **ANSWER:** B
   REFERENCE: OPD, Workplace Clothing, pp. 92–93
   OBJECTIVE: Identify appropriate behavior, attire, attitudes, and social interaction, and other factors that affect job retention and advancement
   STANDARD: CASAS 4.4.1
   OPD TERM: scrubs

7. **ANSWER:** D
   REFERENCE: OPD, Workplace Clothing, pp. 92–93
   OBJECTIVE: Identify common articles of clothing
   STANDARD: CASAS 1.3.9
   OPD TERM: polo shirt

8. **ANSWER:** B
   REFERENCE: OPD, Workplace Clothing, pp. 92–93
   OBJECTIVE: Identify or use appropriate language for informational purposes (e.g., to identify, describe, ask for information, state needs, command, agree or disagree, ask permission)
   STANDARD: CASAS 0.1.2
   OPD TERM: name tag

9. **ANSWER:** D
   REFERENCE: OPD, Workplace Clothing, pp. 92–93
   OBJECTIVE: Identify or use appropriate language for informational purposes (e.g., to identify, describe, ask for information, state needs, command, agree or disagree, ask permission)
   STANDARD: CASAS 0.1.2
   OPD TERM: badge

10. **ANSWER:** A
    REFERENCE: OPD, Workplace Clothing, pp. 92–93
    OBJECTIVE: Identify safe work procedures and common safety equipment, including wearing safe work attire
    STANDARD: CASAS 4.3.3
    OPD TERM: work gloves

Describing Clothes, pp. 43–44

1. **ANSWER:** T
   REFERENCE: OPD, Describing Clothes, pp. 96–97
   OBJECTIVE: Evaluate a situation, statement, or process, assembling information and providing evidence, making judgments, examining assumptions, and identifying contradictions
   STANDARD: CASAS 7.2.5
   OPD TERM: short-sleeved shirt

2. **ANSWER:** B
   REFERENCE: OPD, Describing Clothes, pp. 96–97
   OBJECTIVE: Identify or use appropriate language for informational purposes
   STANDARD: CASAS 0.1.2
   OPD TERM: narrow tie

3. **ANSWER:** D
   REFERENCE: OPD, Describing Clothes, pp. 96–97
   OBJECTIVE: Identify or use appropriate language for informational purposes
   STANDARD: CASAS 0.1.2
   OPD TERM: long skirt

4. **ANSWER:** A
   REFERENCE: OPD, Describing Clothes, pp. 96–97
   OBJECTIVE: Identify or make inferences through inductive and deductive reasoning to hypothesize, predict, conclude, and synthesize; distinguish fact from opinion, and determine what is mandatory and what is discretionary
   STANDARD: CASAS 7.2.4
   OPD TERM: large

5. **ANSWER:** B
   REFERENCE: OPD, Describing Clothes, pp. 96–97
   OBJECTIVE: Identify or make inferences through inductive and deductive reasoning to hypothesize, predict, conclude, and synthesize; distinguish fact from opinion, and determine what is mandatory and what is discretionary
   STANDARD: CASAS 7.2.4
   OPD TERM: it's too small

6. **ANSWER:** A
   REFERENCE: OPD, Describing Clothes, pp. 96–97
   OBJECTIVE: Recognize and/or demonstrate selection and care of clothing and personal property
   STANDARD: CASAS 8.1.4
   OPD TERM: light jacket

7. ANSWER: C
REFERENCE: OPD, Describing Clothes, pp. 96–97
OBJECTIVE: Interpret clothing and pattern sizes and use height and weight tables
STANDARD: CASAS 1.1.9
OPD TERM: medium

8. ANSWER: B
REFERENCE: OPD, Describing Clothes, pp. 96–97
OBJECTIVE: Identify or use appropriate language for informational purposes
STANDARD: CASAS 0.1.2
OPD TERM: short skirt

9. ANSWER: striped
REFERENCE: OPD, Describing Clothes, pp. 96–97
OBJECTIVE: Identify or use appropriate language for informational purposes
STANDARD: CASAS 0.1.2
OPD TERM: striped

10. ANSWER: wide tie
REFERENCE: OPD, Describing Clothes, pp. 96–97
OBJECTIVE: Identify or use appropriate language for informational purposes
STANDARD: CASAS 0.1.2
OPD TERM: wide tie

Doing the Laundry, pp. 45–46

1. ANSWER: B
REFERENCE: OPD, Doing the Laundry, p. 101
OBJECTIVE: Recognize and/or demonstrate laundry skills and related clothing-care skills
STANDARD: CASAS 8.2.4
OPD TERM: laundry detergent

2. ANSWER: D
REFERENCE: OPD, Doing the Laundry, p. 101
OBJECTIVE: Recognize and/or demonstrate laundry skills and related clothing-care skills
STANDARD: CASAS 8.2.4
OPD TERM: laundry

3. ANSWER: C
REFERENCE: OPD, Doing the Laundry, p. 101
OBJECTIVE: Recognize and/or demonstrate laundry skills and related clothing-care skills
STANDARD: CASAS 8.2.4
OPD TERM: ironing board

4. ANSWER: B
REFERENCE: OPD, Doing the Laundry, p. 101
OBJECTIVE: Recognize and/or demonstrate laundry skills and related clothing-care skills
STANDARD: CASAS 8.2.4
OPD TERM: hang up the clothes

5. ANSWER: B
REFERENCE: OPD, Doing the Laundry, p. 101
OBJECTIVE: Recognize and/or demonstrate laundry skills and related clothing-care skills
STANDARD: CASAS 8.2.4
OPD TERM: washer

6. ANSWER: B
REFERENCE: OPD, Doing the Laundry, p. 101
OBJECTIVE: Recognize and/or demonstrate laundry skills and related clothing-care skills
STANDARD: CASAS 8.2.4
OPD TERM: iron

7. ANSWER: D
REFERENCE: OPD, Doing the Laundry, p. 101
OBJECTIVE: Interpret clothing care labels
STANDARD: CASAS 1.7.2
OPD TERM: dryer

8. ANSWER: B
REFERENCE: OPD, Doing the Laundry, p. 101
OBJECTIVE: Recognize and/or demonstrate laundry skills and related clothing-care skills
STANDARD: CASAS 8.2.4
OPD TERM: iron the clothes

9. ANSWER: C
REFERENCE: OPD, Doing the Laundry, p. 101
OBJECTIVE: Recognize and/or demonstrate laundry skills and related clothing-care skills
STANDARD: CASAS 8.2.4
OPD TERM: fold the laundry

10. ANSWER: hanger
REFERENCE: OPD, Doing the Laundry, p. 101
OBJECTIVE: Identify or use appropriate language for informational purposes
STANDARD: CASAS 0.1.2
OPD TERM: hanger

Symptoms and Injuries, pp. 47–48

1. ANSWER: T
REFERENCE: OPD, Symptoms and Injuries, p. 110
OBJECTIVE: Describe symptoms of illness, including identifying parts of the body; interpret doctor's directions
STANDARD: CASAS 3.1.1
OPD TERM: toothache

2. ANSWER: F
REFERENCE: OPD, Symptoms and Injuries, p. 110
OBJECTIVE: Describe symptoms of illness, including identifying parts of the body; interpret doctor's directions
STANDARD: CASAS 3.1.1
OPD TERM: earache

3. ANSWER: D
REFERENCE: OPD, Symptoms and Injuries, p. 110
OBJECTIVE: Describe symptoms of illness, including identifying parts of the body; interpret doctor's directions
STANDARD: CASAS 3.1.1
OPD TERM: backache

4. ANSWER: C
REFERENCE: OPD, Symptoms and Injuries, p. 110
OBJECTIVE: Make comparisons, differentiating among, sorting, and classifying items, information, or ideas
STANDARD: CASAS 7.2.3
OPD TERM: headache

5. ANSWER: D
REFERENCE: OPD, Symptoms and Injuries, p. 110
OBJECTIVE: Identify safety measures that can prevent accidents and injuries
STANDARD: CASAS 3.4.2
OPD TERM: feel dizzy

6. ANSWER: C
REFERENCE: OPD, Symptoms and Injuries, p. 110
OBJECTIVE: Describe symptoms of illness, including identifying parts of the body; interpret doctor's directions
STANDARD: CASAS 3.1.1
OPD TERM: cut

7. ANSWER: C
REFERENCE: OPD, Symptoms and Injuries, p. 110
OBJECTIVE: Describe symptoms of illness, including identifying parts of the body; interpret doctor's directions
STANDARD: CASAS 3.1.1
OPD TERM: sore throat

8. ANSWER: B
REFERENCE: OPD, Symptoms and Injuries, p. 110
OBJECTIVE: Describe symptoms of illness, including identifying parts of the body; interpret doctor's directions
STANDARD: CASAS 3.1.1
OPD TERM: fever

9. ANSWER: A
REFERENCE: OPD, Symptoms and Injuries, p. 110
OBJECTIVE: Describe symptoms of illness, including identifying parts of the body; interpret doctor's directions
STANDARD: CASAS 3.1.1
OPD TERM: feel nauseous

10. ANSWER: stomachache
REFERENCE: OPD, Symptoms and Injuries, p. 110
OBJECTIVE: Describe symptoms of illness, including identifying parts of the body; interpret doctor's directions
STANDARD: CASAS 3.1.1
OPD TERM: stomachache

Illnesses and Medical Conditions, pp. 49–50

1. ANSWER: T
REFERENCE: OPD, Illnesses and Medical Conditions, p. 111
OBJECTIVE: Interpret information about AIDS and other sexually transmitted diseases
STANDARD: CASAS 3.4.4
OPD TERM: HIV (human immunodeficiency virus)

2. ANSWER: F
REFERENCE: OPD, Illnesses and Medical Conditions, p. 111
OBJECTIVE: Describe symptoms of illness, including identifying parts of the body; interpret doctor's directions
STANDARD: CASAS 3.1.1
OPD TERM: heart disease

3. ANSWER: A
REFERENCE: OPD, Illnesses and Medical Conditions, p. 111
OBJECTIVE: Describe symptoms of illness, including identifying parts of the body; interpret doctor's directions
STANDARD: CASAS 3.1.1
OPD TERM: ear infection

4. ANSWER: C
REFERENCE: OPD, Illnesses and Medical Conditions, p. 111
OBJECTIVE: Describe symptoms of illness, including identifying parts of the body; interpret doctor's directions
STANDARD: CASAS 3.1.1
OPD TERM: high blood pressure

5. ANSWER: C
REFERENCE: OPD, Illnesses and Medical Conditions, p. 111
OBJECTIVE: Make comparisons, differentiating among, sorting, and classifying items, information, or ideas
STANDARD: CASAS 7.2.3
OPD TERM: diabetes

6. ANSWER: B
REFERENCE: OPD, Illnesses and Medical Conditions, p. 111
OBJECTIVE: Describe symptoms of illness, including identifying parts of the body; interpret doctor's directions
STANDARD: CASAS 3.1.1
OPD TERM: asthma

7. ANSWER: C
REFERENCE: OPD, Illnesses and Medical
Conditions, p. 111
OBJECTIVE: Describe symptoms of illness,
including identifying parts of the body;
interpret doctor's directions
STANDARD: CASAS 3.1.1
OPD TERM: chicken pox

8. ANSWER: B
REFERENCE: OPD, Illnesses and Medical
Conditions, p. 111
OBJECTIVE: Describe symptoms of illness,
including identifying parts of the body;
interpret doctor's directions
STANDARD: CASAS 3.1.1
OPD TERM: allergies

9. ANSWER: A
REFERENCE: OPD, Illnesses and Medical
Conditions, p. 111
OBJECTIVE: Describe symptoms of illness,
including identifying parts of the body;
interpret doctor's directions
STANDARD: CASAS 3.1.1
OPD TERM: flu

10. ANSWER: C
REFERENCE: OPD, Illnesses and Medical
Conditions, p. 111
OBJECTIVE: Describe symptoms of illness,
including identifying parts of the body;
interpret doctor's directions
STANDARD: CASAS 3.1.1
OPD TERM: cold

A Pharmacy, pp. 51–52

1. ANSWER: T
REFERENCE: OPD, A Pharmacy, pp. 112–113
OBJECTIVE: Interpret medicine labels
STANDARD: CASAS 3.3.2
OPD TERM: prescription label

2. ANSWER: B
REFERENCE: OPD, A Pharmacy, pp. 112–113
OBJECTIVE: Identify and use necessary
medications
STANDARD: CASAS 3.3.1
OPD TERM: eye drops

3. ANSWER: A
REFERENCE: OPD, A Pharmacy, pp. 112–113
OBJECTIVE: Describe symptoms of illness,
including identifying parts of the body;
interpret doctor's directions
STANDARD: CASAS 3.1.1
OPD TERM: prescription

4. ANSWER: D
REFERENCE: OPD, A Pharmacy, pp. 112–113
OBJECTIVE: Interpret medicine labels
STANDARD: CASAS 3.3.2
OPD TERM: capsule

5. ANSWER: B
REFERENCE: OPD, A Pharmacy, pp. 112–113
OBJECTIVE: Identify and use necessary
medications
STANDARD: CASAS 3.3.1
OPD TERM: pain reliever

6. ANSWER: C
REFERENCE: OPD, A Pharmacy, pp. 112–113
OBJECTIVE: Identify and use necessary
medications
STANDARD: CASAS 3.3.1
OPD TERM: antacid

7. ANSWER: C
REFERENCE: OPD, A Pharmacy, pp. 112–113
OBJECTIVE: Identify and use necessary
medications
STANDARD: CASAS 3.3.1
OPD TERM: cough syrup

8. ANSWER: B
REFERENCE: OPD, A Pharmacy, pp. 112–113
OBJECTIVE: Identify the difference between
prescription, over-the-counter, and generic
medications
STANDARD: CASAS 3.3.3
OPD TERM: prescription number

9. ANSWER: B
REFERENCE: OPD, A Pharmacy, pp. 112–113
OBJECTIVE: Identify and use necessary
medications
STANDARD: CASAS 3.3.1
OPD TERM: nasal spray

10. ANSWER: pharmacist
REFERENCE: OPD, A Pharmacy, pp. 112–113
OBJECTIVE: Identify and utilize appropriate
health care services and facilities, including
interacting with providers
STANDARD: CASAS 3.1.3
OPD TERM: pharmacist

Medical Care, pp. 53–54

1. ANSWER: T
REFERENCE: OPD, Medical Care, p. 118
OBJECTIVE: Identify and utilize appropriate
health care services and facilities, including
interacting with providers
STANDARD: CASAS 3.1.3
OPD TERM: check . . . blood pressure

2. ANSWER: F
REFERENCE: OPD, Medical Care, p. 118
OBJECTIVE: Describe symptoms of illness,
including identifying parts of the body;
interpret doctor's directions
STANDARD: CASAS 3.1.1
OPD TERM: examine . . . throat

3. ANSWER: T
REFERENCE: OPD, Medical Care, p. 118
OBJECTIVE: Identify information necessary
to make or keep medical and dental
appointments
STANDARD: CASAS 3.1.2
OPD TERM: appointment

4. ANSWER: F
REFERENCE: OPD, Medical Care, p. 118
OBJECTIVE: Interpret information associated
with medical, dental, or life insurance
STANDARD: CASAS 3.2.3
OPD TERM: health insurance card

5. ANSWER: B
REFERENCE: OPD, Medical Care, p. 118
OBJECTIVE: Describe symptoms of illness,
including identifying parts of the body;
interpret doctor's directions
STANDARD: CASAS 3.1.1
OPD TERM: listen to . . . heart

6. ANSWER: B
REFERENCE: OPD, Medical Care, p. 118
OBJECTIVE: Identify and utilize appropriate
health care services and facilities, including
interacting with providers
STANDARD: CASAS 3.1.3
OPD TERM: draw . . . blood

7. ANSWER: A
REFERENCE: OPD, Medical Care, p. 118
OBJECTIVE: Fill out medical health history forms
STANDARD: CASAS 3.2.1
OPD TERM: health history form

8. ANSWER: C
REFERENCE: OPD, Medical Care, p. 118
OBJECTIVE: Identify and utilize appropriate
health care services and facilities, including
interacting with providers
STANDARD: CASAS 3.1.3
OPD TERM: patient

9. ANSWER: D
REFERENCE: OPD, Medical Care, p. 118
OBJECTIVE: Describe symptoms of illness,
including identifying parts of the body;
interpret doctor's directions
STANDARD: CASAS 3.1.1
OPD TERM: take . . . temperature

10. ANSWER: nurse
REFERENCE: OPD, Medical Care, p. 118
OBJECTIVE: Identify and utilize appropriate
health care services and facilities, including
interacting with providers
STANDARD: CASAS 3.1.3
OPD TERM: nurse

Dental Care, pp. 55–56

1. ANSWER: T
REFERENCE: OPD, Dental Care, p. 119
OBJECTIVE: Identify practices that promote
dental health
STANDARD: CASAS 3.5.4
OPD TERM: braces

2. ANSWER: T
REFERENCE: OPD, Dental Care, p. 119
OBJECTIVE: Identify practices that promote
dental health
STANDARD: CASAS 3.5.4
OPD TERM: decay

3. ANSWER: C
REFERENCE: OPD, Dental Care, p. 119
OBJECTIVE: Identify practices that promote
dental health
STANDARD: CASAS 3.5.4
OPD TERM: take x-rays

4. ANSWER: A
REFERENCE: OPD, Dental Care, p. 119
OBJECTIVE: Describe symptoms of illness,
including identifying parts of the body;
interpret doctor's directions
STANDARD: CASAS 3.1.1
OPD TERM: fill a cavity

5. ANSWER: D
REFERENCE: OPD, Dental Care, p. 119
OBJECTIVE: Identify practices that promote
dental health
STANDARD: CASAS 3.5.4
OPD TERM: dental assistant

6. ANSWER: C
REFERENCE: OPD, Dental Care, p. 119
OBJECTIVE: Identify practices that promote
dental health
STANDARD: CASAS 3.5.4
OPD TERM: clean . . . teeth

7. ANSWER: D
REFERENCE: OPD, Dental Care, p. 119
OBJECTIVE: Describe symptoms of illness,
including identifying parts of the body;
interpret doctor's directions
STANDARD: CASAS 3.1.1
OPD TERM: plaque

8. ANSWER: A
REFERENCE: OPD, Dental Care, p. 119
OBJECTIVE: Describe symptoms of illness,
including identifying parts of the body;
interpret doctor's directions
STANDARD: CASAS 3.1.1
OPD TERM: cavity

9. **ANSWER:** B
   REFERENCE: OPD, Dental Care, p. 119
   OBJECTIVE: Identify and utilize appropriate health care services and facilities, including interacting with providers
   STANDARD: CASAS 3.1.3
   OPD TERM: filling

10. **ANSWER:** dentist
    REFERENCE: OPD, Dental Care, p. 119
    OBJECTIVE: Identify and utilize appropriate health care services and facilities, including interacting with providers
    STANDARD: CASAS 3.1.3
    OPD TERM: dentist

The Bank, pp. 57–58

1. **ANSWER:** F
   REFERENCE: OPD, The Bank, p. 132
   OBJECTIVE: Interpret the procedures and forms associated with banking services, including writing checks
   STANDARD: CASAS 1.8.2
   OPD TERM: withdraw cash

2. **ANSWER:** F
   REFERENCE: OPD, The Bank, p. 132
   OBJECTIVE: Identify common occupations and the skills and education required for them
   STANDARD: CASAS 4.1.8
   OPD TERM: teller

3. **ANSWER:** B
   REFERENCE: OPD, The Bank, p. 132
   OBJECTIVE: Demonstrate the use of savings and checking accounts, including using an ATM
   STANDARD: CASAS 1.8.1
   OPD TERM: check book

4. **ANSWER:** C
   REFERENCE: OPD, The Bank, p. 132
   OBJECTIVE: Demonstrate the use of savings and checking accounts, including using an ATM
   STANDARD: CASAS 1.8.1
   OPD TERM: checking account number

5. **ANSWER:** B
   REFERENCE: OPD, The Bank, p. 132
   OBJECTIVE: Demonstrate the use of savings and checking accounts, including using an ATM
   STANDARD: CASAS 1.8.1
   OPD TERM: balance

6. **ANSWER:** B
   REFERENCE: OPD, The Bank, p. 132
   OBJECTIVE: Demonstrate the use of savings and checking accounts, including using an ATM
   STANDARD: CASAS 1.8.1
   OPD TERM: ATM card

7. **ANSWER:** D
   REFERENCE: OPD, The Bank, p. 132
   OBJECTIVE: Interpret the procedures and forms associated with banking services, including writing checks
   STANDARD: CASAS 1.8.2
   OPD TERM: bank statement

8. **ANSWER:** C
   REFERENCE: OPD, The Bank, p. 132
   OBJECTIVE: Demonstrate the use of savings and checking accounts, including using an ATM
   STANDARD: CASAS 1.8.1
   OPD TERM: make a deposit

9. **ANSWER:** B
   REFERENCE: OPD, The Bank, p. 132
   OBJECTIVE: Identify or make inferences through inductive and deductive reasoning to hypothesize, predict, conclude, and synthesize; distinguish fact from opinion, and determine what is mandatory and what is discretionary
   STANDARD: CASAS 7.2.4
   OPD TERM: cash a check

10. **ANSWER:** customer
    REFERENCE: OPD, The Bank, p. 132
    OBJECTIVE: Demonstrate the use of savings and checking accounts, including using an ATM
    STANDARD: CASAS 1.8.1
    OPD TERM: customer

The Library, pp. 59–60

1. **ANSWER:** C
   REFERENCE: OPD, The Library, p. 133
   OBJECTIVE: Identify common occupations and the skills and education required for them
   STANDARD: CASAS 4.1.8
   OPD TERM: author

2. **ANSWER:** A
   REFERENCE: OPD, The Library, p. 133
   OBJECTIVE: Identify or use appropriate language for informational purposes (e.g., to identify, describe, ask for information, state needs, command, agree or disagree, ask permission)
   STANDARD: CASAS 0.1.2
   OPD TERM: library patron

3. **ANSWER:** A
   REFERENCE: OPD, The Library, p. 133
   OBJECTIVE: Use library services
   STANDARD: CASAS 2.5.6
   OPD TERM: pay a late fine

4. **ANSWER:** C
   REFERENCE: OPD, The Library, p. 133
   OBJECTIVE: Demonstrate ability to use a filing system or other ordered system
   STANDARD: CASAS 4.5.3
   OPD TERM: title

5. **ANSWER:** D
   REFERENCE: OPD, The Library, p. 133
   OBJECTIVE: Converse about daily and leisure activities and personal interests
   STANDARD: CASAS 0.2.4
   OPD TERM: picture book

6. **ANSWER:** C
   REFERENCE: OPD, The Library, p. 133
   OBJECTIVE: Use library services
   STANDARD: CASAS 2.5.6
   OPD TERM: get a library card

7. **ANSWER:** A
   REFERENCE: OPD, The Library, p. 133
   OBJECTIVE: Use library services
   STANDARD: CASAS 2.5.6
   OPD TERM: look for a book

8. **ANSWER:** B
   REFERENCE: OPD, The Library, p. 133
   OBJECTIVE: Use library services
   STANDARD: CASAS 2.5.6
   OPD TERM: return a book

9. **ANSWER:** A
   REFERENCE: OPD, The Library, p. 133
   OBJECTIVE: Use library services
   STANDARD: CASAS 2.5.6
   OPD TERM: check out a book

10. **ANSWER:** clerk
    REFERENCE: OPD, The Library, p. 133
    OBJECTIVE: Identify common occupations and the skills and education required for them
    STANDARD: CASAS 4.1.8
    OPD TERM: library clerk

The Post Office, pp. 61–62

1. **ANSWER:** T
   REFERENCE: OPD, The Post Office, pp. 134–135
   OBJECTIVE: Identify common occupations and the skills and education required for them
   STANDARD: CASAS 4.1.8
   OPD TERM: letter carrier

2. **ANSWER:** T
   REFERENCE: OPD, The Post Office, pp. 134–135
   OBJECTIVE: Identify common occupations and the skills and education required for them
   STANDARD: CASAS 4.1.8
   OPD TERM: postal clerk

3. **ANSWER:** A
   REFERENCE: OPD, The Post Office, pp. 134–135
   OBJECTIVE: Address letters and envelopes
   STANDARD: CASAS 2.4.1
   OPD TERM: address the envelope

4. **ANSWER:** B
   REFERENCE: OPD, The Post Office, pp. 134–135
   OBJECTIVE: Identify or use appropriate language for informational purposes (e.g., to identify, describe, ask for information, state needs, command, agree or disagree, ask permission)
   STANDARD: CASAS 0.1.2
   OPD TERM: letter

5. **ANSWER:** B
   REFERENCE: OPD, The Post Office, pp. 134–135
   OBJECTIVE: Purchase stamps and other postal items and services
   STANDARD: CASAS 2.4.4
   OPD TERM: stamp

6. **ANSWER:** B
   REFERENCE: OPD, The Post Office, pp. 134–135
   OBJECTIVE: Interpret or write a personal note, invitation, or letter
   STANDARD: CASAS 0.2.3
   OPD TERM: greeting card

7. **ANSWER:** D
   REFERENCE: OPD, The Post Office, pp. 134–135
   OBJECTIVE: Purchase stamps and other postal items and services
   STANDARD: CASAS 2.4.4
   OPD TERM: package

8. **ANSWER:** B
   REFERENCE: OPD, The Post Office, pp. 134–135
   OBJECTIVE: Interpret postal rates and types of mailing services
   STANDARD: CASAS 2.4.2
   OPD TERM: book of stamps

9. **ANSWER:** post card
   REFERENCE: OPD, The Post Office, pp. 134–135
   OBJECTIVE: Interpret or write a personal note, invitation, or letter
   STANDARD: CASAS 0.2.3
   OPD TERM: post card

10. **ANSWER:** envelope
    REFERENCE: OPD, The Post Office, pp. 134–135
    OBJECTIVE: Identify or use appropriate language for informational purposes (e.g., to identify, describe, ask for information, state needs, command, agree or disagree, ask permission)
    STANDARD: CASAS 0.1.2
    OPD TERM: envelope

Department of Motor Vehicles (DMV), pp. 63–64

1. **ANSWER:** F
   REFERENCE: OPD, Department of Motor Vehicles (DMV), pp. 136–137
   OBJECTIVE: Interpret permit and license requirements
   STANDARD: CASAS 2.5.7
   OPD TERM: get your license

2. **ANSWER:** T
   REFERENCE: OPD, Department of Motor Vehicles (DMV), pp. 136–137
   OBJECTIVE: Identify driving regulations and procedures to obtain a driver's license
   STANDARD: CASAS 1.9.2
   OPD TERM: pass a driving test

3. **ANSWER:** D
   REFERENCE: OPD, Department of Motor Vehicles (DMV), pp. 136–137
   OBJECTIVE: Identify driving regulations and procedures to obtain a driver's license
   STANDARD: CASAS 1.9.2
   OPD TERM: take a written test

4. **ANSWER:** B
   REFERENCE: OPD, Department of Motor Vehicles (DMV), pp. 136–137
   OBJECTIVE: Identify driving regulations and procedures to obtain a driver's license
   STANDARD: CASAS 1.9.2
   OPD TERM: take a driver education course

5. **ANSWER:** C
   REFERENCE: OPD, Department of Motor Vehicles (DMV), pp. 136–137
   OBJECTIVE: Evaluate a situation, statement, or process, assembling information and providing evidence, making judgments, examining assumptions, and identifying contradictions
   STANDARD: CASAS 7.2.5
   OPD TERM: pay the application fee

6. **ANSWER:** A
   REFERENCE: OPD, Department of Motor Vehicles (DMV), pp. 136–137
   OBJECTIVE: Identify driving regulations and procedures to obtain a driver's license
   STANDARD: CASAS 1.9.2
   OPD TERM: fingerprint

7. **ANSWER:** A
   REFERENCE: OPD, Department of Motor Vehicles (DMV), pp. 136–137
   OBJECTIVE: Interpret information related to the selection and purchase of a car
   STANDARD: CASAS 1.9.5
   OPD TERM: registration tag

8. **ANSWER:** B
   REFERENCE: OPD, Department of Motor Vehicles (DMV), pp. 136–137
   OBJECTIVE: Identify or use appropriate language for informational purposes (e.g., to identify, describe, ask for information, state needs, command, agree or disagree, ask permission)
   STANDARD: CASAS 0.1.2
   OPD TERM: window

9. **ANSWER:** C
   REFERENCE: OPD, Department of Motor Vehicles (DMV), pp. 136–137
   OBJECTIVE: Identify driving regulations and procedures to obtain a driver's license
   STANDARD: CASAS 1.9.2
   OPD TERM: driver's license

10. **ANSWER:** D
    REFERENCE: OPD, Department of Motor Vehicles (DMV), pp. 136–137
    OBJECTIVE: Identify or use appropriate language for informational purposes (e.g., to identify, describe, ask for information, state needs, command, agree or disagree, ask permission)
    STANDARD: CASAS 0.1.2
    OPD TERM: driver's license number

11. **ANSWER:** B
    REFERENCE: OPD, Department of Motor Vehicles (DMV), pp. 136–137
    OBJECTIVE: Identify or use appropriate language for informational purposes (e.g., to identify, describe, ask for information, state needs, command, agree or disagree, ask permission)
    STANDARD: CASAS 0.1.2
    OPD TERM: license plate

12. **ANSWER:** DMV clerk
    REFERENCE: OPD, Department of Motor Vehicles (DMV), pp. 136–137
    OBJECTIVE: Identify common occupations and the skills and education required for them
    STANDARD: CASAS 4.1.8
    OPD TERM: DMV clerk

13. **ANSWER:** vision exam
    REFERENCE: OPD, Department of Motor Vehicles (DMV), pp. 136–137
    OBJECTIVE: Identify or make inferences through inductive and deductive reasoning to hypothesize, predict, conclude, and synthesize; distinguish fact from opinion, and determine what is mandatory and what is discretionary
    STANDARD: CASAS 7.2.4
    OPD TERM: vision exam

14. **ANSWER:** photo
    REFERENCE: OPD, Department of Motor Vehicles (DMV), pp. 136–137
    OBJECTIVE: Identify or use appropriate language for informational purposes (e.g., to identify, describe, ask for information, state needs, command, agree or disagree, ask permission)
    STANDARD: CASAS 0.1.2
    OPD TERM: photo

15. **ANSWER:** insurance
    REFERENCE: OPD, Department of Motor Vehicles (DMV), pp. 136–137
    OBJECTIVE: Interpret information about automobile insurance
    STANDARD: CASAS 1.9.8
    OPD TERM: proof of insurance

Government and Military Service, pp. 65–66

1. **ANSWER:** T
   REFERENCE: OPD, Government and Military Service, pp. 138–139
   OBJECTIVE: Identify local, state and federal government leaders
   STANDARD: CASAS 5.5.8
   OPD TERM: governor

2. **ANSWER:** T
   REFERENCE: OPD, Government and Military Service, pp. 138–139
   OBJECTIVE: Identify local, state and federal government leaders
   STANDARD: CASAS 5.5.8
   OPD TERM: mayor

3. **ANSWER:** T
   REFERENCE: OPD, Government and Military Service, pp. 138–139
   OBJECTIVE: Identify local, state and federal government leaders
   STANDARD: CASAS 5.5.8
   OPD TERM: state capital

4. **ANSWER:** B
   REFERENCE: OPD, Government and Military Service, pp. 138–139
   OBJECTIVE: Interpret information about executive activities
   STANDARD: CASAS 5.5.4
   OPD TERM: White House

5. **ANSWER:** C
   REFERENCE: OPD, Government and Military Service, pp. 138–139
   OBJECTIVE: Interpret information about executive activities
   STANDARD: CASAS 5.5.4
   OPD TERM: president

6. **ANSWER:** C
   REFERENCE: OPD, Government and Military Service, pp. 138–139
   OBJECTIVE: Interpret information about judicial activities
   STANDARD: CASAS 5.5.3
   OPD TERM: chief justice

7. **ANSWER:** D
   REFERENCE: OPD, Government and Military Service, pp. 138–139
   OBJECTIVE: Make comparisons, differentiating among, sorting, and classifying items, information, or ideas
   STANDARD: CASAS 7.2.3
   OPD TERM: Supreme Court

8. **ANSWER:** A
   REFERENCE: OPD, Government and Military Service, pp. 138–139
   OBJECTIVE: Identify local, state and federal government leaders
   STANDARD: CASAS 5.5.8
   OPD TERM: Legislature

9. **ANSWER:** B
   REFERENCE: OPD, Government and Military Service, pp. 138–139
   OBJECTIVE: Interpret information about military activities
   STANDARD: CASAS 5.5.5
   OPD TERM: Navy

10. **ANSWER:** C
    REFERENCE: OPD, Government and Military Service, pp. 138–139
    OBJECTIVE: Interpret information about military activities
    STANDARD: CASAS 5.5.5
    OPD TERM: Air Force

11. **ANSWER:** Army
    REFERENCE: OPD, Government and Military Service, pp. 138–139
    OBJECTIVE: Interpret information about military activities
    STANDARD: CASAS 5.5.5
    OPD TERM: Army

12. **ANSWER:** Congress
    REFERENCE: OPD, Government and Military Service, pp. 138–139
    OBJECTIVE: Interpret information about legislative activities
    STANDARD: CASAS 5.5.2
    OPD TERM: Congress

13. **ANSWER:** U.S. Capitol
REFERENCE: OPD, Government and Military Service, pp. 138–139
OBJECTIVE: Interpret information about legislative activities
STANDARD: CASAS 5.5.2
OPD TERM: U.S. Capitol

14. **ANSWER:** city council
REFERENCE: OPD, Government and Military Service, pp. 138–139
OBJECTIVE: Identify local, state and federal government leaders
STANDARD: CASAS 5.5.8
OPD TERM: city council

15. **ANSWER:** councilperson
REFERENCE: OPD, Government and Military Service, pp. 138–139
OBJECTIVE: Interpret information about legislative activities
STANDARD: CASAS 5.5.2
OPD TERM: councilperson

Public Safety, pp. 67–68

1. **ANSWER:** T
REFERENCE: OPD, Public Safety, p. 143
OBJECTIVE: Identify safety measures that can prevent accidents and injuries
STANDARD: CASAS 3.4.2
OPD TERM: lock your doors

2. **ANSWER:** B
REFERENCE: OPD, Public Safety, p. 143
OBJECTIVE: Recognize problems related to drugs, tobacco, and alcohol, and identify where treatment may be obtained
STANDARD: CASAS 3.4.5
OPD TERM: don't drink and drive

3. **ANSWER:** C
REFERENCE: OPD, Public Safety, p. 143
OBJECTIVE: Identify procedures for reporting a crime
STANDARD: CASAS 5.3.8
OPD TERM: report crimes to the police

4. **ANSWER:** C
REFERENCE: OPD, Public Safety, p. 143
OBJECTIVE: Identify safety measures that can prevent accidents and injuries
STANDARD: CASAS 3.4.2
OPD TERM: walk with a friend

5. **ANSWER:** A
REFERENCE: OPD, Public Safety, p. 143
OBJECTIVE: Identify safety measures that can prevent accidents and injuries
STANDARD: CASAS 3.4.2
OPD TERM: protect your purse or wallet

6. **ANSWER:** A
REFERENCE: OPD, Public Safety, p. 143
OBJECTIVE: Identify safety measures that can prevent accidents and injuries
STANDARD: CASAS 3.4.2
OPD TERM: don't open your door to strangers

7. **ANSWER:** B
REFERENCE: OPD, Public Safety, p. 143
OBJECTIVE: Identify safety measures that can prevent accidents and injuries
STANDARD: CASAS 3.4.2
OPD TERM: shop on secure websites

8. **ANSWER:** C
REFERENCE: OPD, Public Safety, p. 143
OBJECTIVE: Identify safety measures that can prevent accidents and injuries
STANDARD: CASAS 3.4.2
OPD TERM: join a Neighborhood Watch

9. **ANSWER:** B
REFERENCE: OPD, Public Safety, p. 143
OBJECTIVE: Identify safety measures that can prevent accidents and injuries
STANDARD: CASAS 3.4.2
OPD TERM: conceal your PIN number

10. **ANSWER:** D
REFERENCE: OPD, Public Safety, p. 143
OBJECTIVE: Identify safety measures that can prevent accidents and injuries
STANDARD: CASAS 3.4.2
OPD TERM: be aware of your surroundings

Emergency Procedures, pp. 69–70

1. **ANSWER:** F
REFERENCE: OPD, Emergency Procedures, pp. 146–147
OBJECTIVE: Identify safety measures that can prevent accidents and injuries
STANDARD: CASAS 3.4.2
OPD TERM: follow directions

2. **ANSWER:** F
REFERENCE: OPD, Emergency Procedures, pp. 146–147
OBJECTIVE: Recognize and evaluate logical statements
STANDARD: CASAS 6.5.4
OPD TERM: watch the weather

3. **ANSWER:** T
REFERENCE: OPD, Emergency Procedures, pp. 146–147
OBJECTIVE: Recognize and evaluate logical statements
STANDARD: CASAS 6.5.4
OPD TERM: pay attention to warnings

4. **ANSWER:** A
REFERENCE: OPD, Emergency Procedures, pp. 146–147
OBJECTIVE: Evaluate a situation, statement, or process, assembling information and providing evidence, making judgments, examining assumptions, and identifying contradictions
STANDARD: CASAS 7.2.5
OPD TERM: remain calm

5. **ANSWER:** C
REFERENCE: OPD, Emergency Procedures, pp. 146–147
OBJECTIVE: Evaluate a situation, statement, or process, assembling information and providing evidence, making judgments, examining assumptions, and identifying contradictions
STANDARD: CASAS 7.2.5
OPD TERM: clean up debris

6. **ANSWER:** A
REFERENCE: OPD, Emergency Procedures, pp. 146–147
OBJECTIVE: Evaluate a situation, statement, or process, assembling information and providing evidence, making judgments, examining assumptions, and identifying contradictions
STANDARD: CASAS 7.2.5
OPD TERM: inspect utilities

7. **ANSWER:** A
REFERENCE: OPD, Emergency Procedures, pp. 146–147
OBJECTIVE: Interpret procedures for simple first-aid
STANDARD: CASAS 3.4.3
OPD TERM: first aid kit

8. **ANSWER:** C
REFERENCE: OPD, Emergency Procedures, pp. 146–147
OBJECTIVE: Identify safety measures that can prevent accidents and injuries
STANDARD: CASAS 3.4.2
OPD TERM: make a disaster kit

9. **ANSWER:** B
REFERENCE: OPD, Emergency Procedures, pp. 146–147
OBJECTIVE: Evaluate a situation, statement, or process, assembling information and providing evidence, making judgments, examining assumptions, and identifying contradictions
STANDARD: CASAS 7.2.5
OPD TERM: warm clothes

10. **ANSWER:** D
REFERENCE: OPD, Emergency Procedures, pp. 146–147
OBJECTIVE: Evaluate a situation, statement, or process, assembling information and providing evidence, making judgments, examining assumptions, and identifying contradictions
STANDARD: CASAS 7.2.5
OPD TERM: blankets

11. **ANSWER:** A
REFERENCE: OPD, Emergency Procedures, pp. 146–147
OBJECTIVE: Evaluate a situation, statement, or process, assembling information and providing evidence, making judgments, examining assumptions, and identifying contradictions
STANDARD: CASAS 7.2.5
OPD TERM: canned food

12. **ANSWER:** flashlight
REFERENCE: OPD, Emergency Procedures, pp. 146–147
OBJECTIVE: Evaluate a situation, statement, or process, assembling information and providing evidence, making judgments, examining assumptions, and identifying contradictions
STANDARD: CASAS 7.2.5
OPD TERM: flashlight

13. **ANSWER:** batteries
REFERENCE: OPD, Emergency Procedures, pp. 146–147
OBJECTIVE: Evaluate a situation, statement, or process, assembling information and providing evidence, making judgments, examining assumptions, and identifying contradictions
STANDARD: CASAS 7.2.5
OPD TERM: batteries

14. **ANSWER:** bottled water
REFERENCE: OPD, Emergency Procedures, pp. 146–147
OBJECTIVE: Evaluate a situation, statement, or process, assembling information and providing evidence, making judgments, examining assumptions, and identifying contradictions
STANDARD: CASAS 7.2.5
OPD TERM: bottled water

15. **ANSWER:** can opener
REFERENCE: OPD, Emergency Procedures, pp. 146–147
OBJECTIVE: Evaluate a situation, statement, or process, assembling information and providing evidence, making judgments, examining assumptions, and identifying contradictions
STANDARD: CASAS 7.2.5
OPD TERM: can opener

Traffic Signs, pp. 71–72

1. **ANSWER:** T
   REFERENCE: OPD, Traffic Signs, p. 154
   OBJECTIVE: Recognize and use signs related to transportation
   STANDARD: CASAS 2.2.2
   OPD TERM: handicapped parking

2. **ANSWER:** F
   REFERENCE: OPD, Traffic Signs, p. 154
   OBJECTIVE: Recognize and use signs related to transportation
   STANDARD: CASAS 2.2.2
   OPD TERM: no left turn

3. **ANSWER:** T
   REFERENCE: OPD, Traffic Signs, p. 154
   OBJECTIVE: Recognize and use signs related to transportation
   STANDARD: CASAS 2.2.2
   OPD TERM: pedestrian crossing

4. **ANSWER:** A
   REFERENCE: OPD, Traffic Signs, p. 154
   OBJECTIVE: Interpret highway and traffic signs
   STANDARD: CASAS 1.9.1
   OPD TERM: do not enter

5. **ANSWER:** D
   REFERENCE: OPD, Traffic Signs, p. 154
   OBJECTIVE: Recognize and use signs related to transportation
   STANDARD: CASAS 2.2.2
   OPD TERM: one way

6. **ANSWER:** A
   REFERENCE: OPD, Traffic Signs, p. 154
   OBJECTIVE: Interpret highway and traffic signs
   STANDARD: CASAS 1.9.1
   OPD TERM: speed limit

7. **ANSWER:** C
   REFERENCE: OPD, Traffic Signs, p. 154
   OBJECTIVE: Recognize and use signs related to transportation
   STANDARD: CASAS 2.2.2
   OPD TERM: no parking

8. **ANSWER:** C
   REFERENCE: OPD, Traffic Signs, p. 154
   OBJECTIVE: Recognize and use signs related to transportation
   STANDARD: CASAS 2.2.2
   OPD TERM: right turn only

9. **ANSWER:** stop
   REFERENCE: OPD, Traffic Signs, p. 154
   OBJECTIVE: Interpret highway and traffic signs
   STANDARD: CASAS 1.9.1
   OPD TERM: stop

10. **ANSWER:** yield
    REFERENCE: OPD, Traffic Signs, p. 154
    OBJECTIVE: Recognize and use signs related to transportation
    STANDARD: CASAS 2.2.2
    OPD TERM: yield

Directions and Maps, pp. 73–74

1. **ANSWER:** F
   REFERENCE: OPD, Directions and Maps, p. 155
   OBJECTIVE: Identify or make inferences through inductive and deductive reasoning to hypothesize, predict, conclude, and synthesize; distinguish fact from opinion, and determine what is mandatory and what is discretionary
   STANDARD: CASAS 7.2.4
   OPD TERM: Internet map

2. **ANSWER:** T
   REFERENCE: OPD, Directions and Maps, p. 155
   OBJECTIVE: Use or interpret measurement instruments, such as rulers, scales, gauges, and dials
   STANDARD: CASAS 6.6.4
   OPD TERM: scale

3. **ANSWER:** D
   REFERENCE: OPD, Directions and Maps, p. 155
   OBJECTIVE: Identify or use appropriate language for informational purposes (e.g., to identify, describe, ask for information, state needs, command, agree or disagree, ask permission)
   STANDARD: CASAS 0.1.2
   OPD TERM: go straight

4. **ANSWER:** D
   REFERENCE: OPD, Directions and Maps, p. 155
   OBJECTIVE: Interpret maps related to driving
   STANDARD: CASAS 1.9.4
   OPD TERM: west

5. **ANSWER:** B
   REFERENCE: OPD, Directions and Maps, p. 155
   OBJECTIVE: Interpret highway and traffic signs
   STANDARD: CASAS 1.9.1
   OPD TERM: turn left

6. **ANSWER:** A
   REFERENCE: OPD, Directions and Maps, p. 155
   OBJECTIVE: Use maps relating to travel needs
   STANDARD: CASAS 2.2.5
   OPD TERM: north

7. **ANSWER:** C
   REFERENCE: OPD, Directions and Maps, p. 155
   OBJECTIVE: Identify or make inferences through inductive and deductive reasoning to hypothesize, predict, conclude, and synthesize; distinguish fact from opinion, and determine what is mandatory and what is discretionary
   STANDARD: CASAS 7.2.4
   OPD TERM: east

8. **ANSWER:** C
   REFERENCE: OPD, Directions and Maps, p. 155
   OBJECTIVE: Interpret highway and traffic signs
   STANDARD: CASAS 1.9.1
   OPD TERM: turn right

9. **ANSWER:** A
   REFERENCE: OPD, Directions and Maps, p. 155
   OBJECTIVE: Interpret highway and traffic signs
   STANDARD: CASAS 1.9.1
   OPD TERM: stop at the corner

10. **ANSWER:** B
    REFERENCE: OPD, Directions and Maps, p. 155
    OBJECTIVE: Ask for, give, follow, or clarify directions
    STANDARD: CASAS 2.2.1
    OPD TERM: south

Buying and Maintaining a Car, pp. 75–76

1. **ANSWER:** T
   REFERENCE: OPD, Buying and Maintaining a Car, p. 157
   OBJECTIVE: Interpret information related to automobile maintenance
   STANDARD: CASAS 1.9.6
   OPD TERM: check the oil

2. **ANSWER:** F
   REFERENCE: OPD, Buying and Maintaining a Car, p. 157
   OBJECTIVE: Interpret information related to automobile maintenance
   STANDARD: CASAS 1.9.6
   OPD TERM: register the car

3. **ANSWER:** D
   REFERENCE: OPD, Buying and Maintaining a Car, p. 157
   OBJECTIVE: Interpret information related to automobile maintenance
   STANDARD: CASAS 1.9.6
   OPD TERM: take the car to a mechanic

4. **ANSWER:** C
   REFERENCE: OPD, Buying and Maintaining a Car, p. 157
   OBJECTIVE: Interpret information related to automobile maintenance
   STANDARD: CASAS 1.9.6
   OPD TERM: get the title from the seller

5. **ANSWER:** D
   REFERENCE: OPD, Buying and Maintaining a Car, p. 157
   OBJECTIVE: Interpret information related to the selection and purchase of a car
   STANDARD: CASAS 1.9.5
   OPD TERM: look at car ads

6. **ANSWER:** C
   REFERENCE: OPD, Buying and Maintaining a Car, p. 157
   OBJECTIVE: Interpret information related to automobile maintenance
   STANDARD: CASAS 1.9.6
   OPD TERM: put in coolant

7. **ANSWER:** B
   REFERENCE: OPD, Buying and Maintaining a Car, p. 157
   OBJECTIVE: Interpret information related to the selection and purchase of a car
   STANDARD: CASAS 1.9.5
   OPD TERM: ask the seller about the car

8. **ANSWER:** A
   REFERENCE: OPD, Buying and Maintaining a Car, p. 157
   OBJECTIVE: Interpret information related to the selection and purchase of a car
   STANDARD: CASAS 1.9.5
   OPD TERM: negotiate a price

9. **ANSWER:** B
   REFERENCE: OPD, Buying and Maintaining a Car, p. 157
   OBJECTIVE: Interpret information related to automobile maintenance
   STANDARD: CASAS 1.9.6
   OPD TERM: fill the tank with gas

10. **ANSWER:** A
    REFERENCE: OPD, Buying and Maintaining a Car, p. 157
    OBJECTIVE: Interpret information related to automobile maintenance
    STANDARD: CASAS 1.9.6
    OPD TERM: go for a smog check

The Workplace, pp. 77–78

1. **ANSWER:** F
   REFERENCE: OPD, The Workplace, pp. 164–165
   OBJECTIVE: Identify common occupations and the skills and education required for them
   STANDARD: CASAS 4.1.8
   OPD TERM: office

2. **ANSWER:** T
   REFERENCE: OPD, The Workplace, pp. 164–165
   OBJECTIVE: Interpret general work-related vocabulary (e.g., experience, swing shift)
   STANDARD: CASAS 4.1.6
   OPD TERM: deductions

3. **ANSWER:** C
   REFERENCE: OPD, The Workplace, pp. 164–165
   OBJECTIVE: Identify common occupations and the skills and education required for them
   STANDARD: CASAS 4.1.8
   OPD TERM: receptionist

4. **ANSWER:** D
   REFERENCE: OPD, The Workplace, pp. 164–165
   OBJECTIVE: Interpret general work-related vocabulary (e.g., experience, swing shift)
   STANDARD: CASAS 4.1.6
   OPD TERM: employee

5. **ANSWER:** B
   REFERENCE: OPD, The Workplace, pp. 164–165
   OBJECTIVE: Interpret general work-related vocabulary (e.g., experience, swing shift)
   STANDARD: CASAS 4.1.6
   OPD TERM: entrance

6. **ANSWER:** D
   REFERENCE: OPD, The Workplace, pp. 164–165
   OBJECTIVE: Identify common occupations and the skills and education required for them
   STANDARD: CASAS 4.1.8
   OPD TERM: payroll clerk

7. **ANSWER:** C
   REFERENCE: OPD, The Workplace, pp. 164–165
   OBJECTIVE: Interpret general work-related vocabulary (e.g., experience, swing shift)
   STANDARD: CASAS 4.1.6
   OPD TERM: wages

8. **ANSWER:** B
   REFERENCE: OPD, The Workplace, pp. 164–165
   OBJECTIVE: Interpret general work-related vocabulary (e.g., experience, swing shift)
   STANDARD: CASAS 4.1.6
   OPD TERM: employer

9. **ANSWER:** A
   REFERENCE: OPD, The Workplace, pp. 164–165
   OBJECTIVE: Interpret general work-related vocabulary (e.g., experience, swing shift)
   STANDARD: CASAS 4.1.6
   OPD TERM: paycheck

10. **ANSWER:** time clock
    REFERENCE: OPD, The Workplace, pp. 164–165
    OBJECTIVE: Interpret general work-related vocabulary (e.g., experience, swing shift)
    STANDARD: CASAS 4.1.6
    OPD TERM: time clock

Office Skills, pp. 79–80

1. **ANSWER:** F
   REFERENCE: OPD, Office Skills, p. 171
   OBJECTIVE: Demonstrate use of common business machines
   STANDARD: CASAS 4.5.4
   OPD TERM: take dictation

2. **ANSWER:** T
   REFERENCE: OPD, Office Skills, p. 171
   OBJECTIVE: Identify common tools, equipment, machines, and materials required for one's job
   STANDARD: CASAS 4.5.1
   OPD TERM: staple

3. **ANSWER:** A
   REFERENCE: OPD, Office Skills, p. 171
   OBJECTIVE: Identify common tools, equipment, machines, and materials required for one's job
   STANDARD: CASAS 4.5.1
   OPD TERM: type a letter

4. **ANSWER:** B
   REFERENCE: OPD, Office Skills, p. 171
   OBJECTIVE: Interpret general work-related vocabulary (e.g., experience, swing shift)
   STANDARD: CASAS 4.1.6
   OPD TERM: print a document

5. **ANSWER:** A
   REFERENCE: OPD, Office Skills, p. 171
   OBJECTIVE: Demonstrate use of common business machines
   STANDARD: CASAS 4.5.4
   OPD TERM: enter data

6. **ANSWER:** D
   REFERENCE: OPD, Office Skills, p. 171
   OBJECTIVE: Interpret general work-related vocabulary (e.g., experience, swing shift)
   STANDARD: CASAS 4.1.6
   OPD TERM: check messages

7. **ANSWER:** C
   REFERENCE: OPD, Office Skills, p. 171
   OBJECTIVE: Interpret general work-related vocabulary (e.g., experience, swing shift)
   STANDARD: CASAS 4.1.6
   OPD TERM: leave a message

8. **ANSWER:** B
   REFERENCE: OPD, Office Skills, p. 171
   OBJECTIVE: Interpret general work-related vocabulary (e.g., experience, swing shift)
   STANDARD: CASAS 4.1.6
   OPD TERM: take a message

9. **ANSWER:** make copies
   REFERENCE: OPD, Office Skills, p. 171
   OBJECTIVE: Demonstrate ability to select, set up, and use tools and machines in order to accomplish a task, while operating within a technological system
   STANDARD: CASAS 4.5.6
   OPD TERM: make copies

10. **ANSWER:** fax
    REFERENCE: OPD, Office Skills, p. 171
    OBJECTIVE: Demonstrate use of common business machines
    STANDARD: CASAS 4.5.4
    OPD TERM: fax a document

Career Planning, pp. 81–82

1. **ANSWER:** F
   REFERENCE: OPD, Career Planning, p. 172
   OBJECTIVE: Identify and use information about training opportunities
   STANDARD: CASAS 4.1.4
   OPD TERM: vocational training

2. **ANSWER:** T
   REFERENCE: OPD, Career Planning, p. 172
   OBJECTIVE: Identify and use information about training opportunities
   STANDARD: CASAS 4.1.4
   OPD TERM: training

3. **ANSWER:** B
   REFERENCE: OPD, Career Planning, p. 172
   OBJECTIVE: Identify and use sources of information about job opportunities such as job descriptions, job ads, and announcements, and about the workforce and job market
   STANDARD: CASAS 4.1.3
   OPD TERM: job fair

4. **ANSWER:** D
   REFERENCE: OPD, Career Planning, p. 172
   OBJECTIVE: Identify procedures for career planning, including self-assessment
   STANDARD: CASAS 4.1.9
   OPD TERM: career counselor

5. **ANSWER:** A
   REFERENCE: OPD, Career Planning, p. 172
   OBJECTIVE: Identify appropriate skills and education for keeping a job and getting a promotion
   STANDARD: CASAS 4.4.2
   OPD TERM: internship

6. **ANSWER:** C
   REFERENCE: OPD, Career Planning, p. 172
   OBJECTIVE: Interpret general work-related vocabulary (e.g., experience, swing shift)
   STANDARD: CASAS 4.1.6
   OPD TERM: promotion

7. **ANSWER:** B
   REFERENCE: OPD, Career Planning, p. 172
   OBJECTIVE: Interpret general work-related vocabulary (e.g., experience, swing shift)
   STANDARD: CASAS 4.1.6
   OPD TERM: on-the-job training

8. **ANSWER:** D
   REFERENCE: OPD, Career Planning, p. 172
   OBJECTIVE: Identify procedures for career planning, including self-assessment
   STANDARD: CASAS 4.1.9
   OPD TERM: resource center

9. **ANSWER:** A
   REFERENCE: OPD, Career Planning, p. 172
   OBJECTIVE: Interpret general work-related vocabulary (e.g., experience, swing shift)
   STANDARD: CASAS 4.1.6
   OPD TERM: entry-level job

10. **ANSWER:** B
    REFERENCE: OPD, Career Planning, p. 172
    OBJECTIVE: Interpret general work-related vocabulary (e.g., experience, swing shift)
    STANDARD: CASAS 4.1.6
    OPD TERM: new job

Job Search, pp. 83–84

1. **ANSWER:** T
   REFERENCE: OPD, Job Search, p. 173
   OBJECTIVE: Identify and use sources of information about job opportunities such as job descriptions, job ads, and announcements, and about the workforce and job market
   STANDARD: CASAS 4.1.3
   OPD TERM: look in the classifieds

2. **ANSWER:** F
   REFERENCE: OPD, Job Search, p. 173
   OBJECTIVE: Follow procedures for applying for a job, including interpreting and completing job applications, resumes, and letters of application
   STANDARD: CASAS 4.1.2
   OPD TERM: write a cover letter

3. **ANSWER:** C
   REFERENCE: OPD, Job Search, p. 173
   OBJECTIVE: Follow procedures for applying for a job, including interpreting and completing job applications, resumes, and letters of application
   STANDARD: CASAS 4.1.2
   OPD TERM: set up an interview

4. **ANSWER:** B
   REFERENCE: OPD, Job Search, p. 173
   OBJECTIVE: Identify and use sources of information about job opportunities such as job descriptions, job ads and announcements, and about the workforce and job market
   STANDARD: CASAS 4.1.3
   OPD TERM: go on an interview

5. **ANSWER:** D
   REFERENCE: OPD, Job Search, p. 173
   OBJECTIVE: Identify appropriate behavior and attitudes for getting a job
   STANDARD: CASAS 4.1.7
   OPD TERM: get hired

6. **ANSWER:** B
   REFERENCE: OPD, Job Search, p. 173
   OBJECTIVE: Follow procedures for applying for a job, including interpreting and completing job applications, resumes, and letters of application
   STANDARD: CASAS 4.1.2
   OPD TERM: write a resume

7. **ANSWER:** D
   REFERENCE: OPD, Job Search, p. 173
   OBJECTIVE: Identify and use sources of information about job opportunities such as job descriptions, job ads, and announcements, and about the workforce and job market
   STANDARD: CASAS 4.1.3
   OPD TERM: check Internet job sites

8. **ANSWER:** B
   REFERENCE: OPD, Job Search, p. 173
   OBJECTIVE: Follow procedures for applying for a job, including interpreting and completing job applications, resumes, and letters of application
   STANDARD: CASAS 4.1.2
   OPD TERM: fill out an application

9. **ANSWER:** B
   REFERENCE: OPD, Job Search, p. 173
   OBJECTIVE: Identify and use sources of information about job opportunities such as job descriptions, job ads and announcements, and about the workforce and job market
   STANDARD: CASAS 4.1.3
   OPD TERM: talk to friends

10. **ANSWER:** C
    REFERENCE: OPD, Job Search, p. 173
    OBJECTIVE: Identify and use sources of information about job opportunities such as job descriptions, job ads and announcements, and about the workforce and job market
    STANDARD: CASAS 4.1.3
    OPD TERM: look for help wanted signs

Interview Skills, pp. 85–86

1. **ANSWER:** F
   REFERENCE: OPD, Interview Skills, p. 174
   OBJECTIVE: Identify appropriate behavior and attitudes for getting a job
   STANDARD: CASAS 4.1.7
   OPD TERM: turn off your cell phone

2. **ANSWER:** T
   REFERENCE: OPD, Interview Skills, p. 174
   OBJECTIVE: Identify procedures involved in interviewing for a job, such as arranging for an interview, acting and dressing appropriately, and selecting appropriate questions and responses
   STANDARD: CASAS 4.1.5
   OPD TERM: don't be late

3. **ANSWER:** D
   REFERENCE: OPD, Interview Skills, p. 174
   OBJECTIVE: Identify appropriate behavior and attitudes for getting a job
   STANDARD: CASAS 4.1.7
   OPD TERM: listen carefully

4. **ANSWER:** B
   REFERENCE: OPD, Interview Skills, p. 174
   OBJECTIVE: Identify procedures involved in interviewing for a job, such as arranging for an interview, acting and dressing appropriately, and selecting appropriate questions and responses
   STANDARD: CASAS 4.1.5
   OPD TERM: prepare for the interview

5. **ANSWER:** A
   REFERENCE: OPD, Interview Skills, p. 174
   OBJECTIVE: Identify appropriate behavior and attitudes for getting a job
   STANDARD: CASAS 4.1.7
   OPD TERM: write a thank-you note

6. **ANSWER:** C
   REFERENCE: OPD, Interview Skills, p. 174
   OBJECTIVE: Identify procedures involved in interviewing for a job, such as arranging for an interview, acting and dressing appropriately, and selecting appropriate questions and responses
   STANDARD: CASAS 4.1.5
   OPD TERM: ask questions

7. **ANSWER:** C
   REFERENCE: OPD, Interview Skills, p. 174
   OBJECTIVE: Identify procedures involved in interviewing for a job, such as arranging for an interview, acting and dressing appropriately, and selecting appropriate questions and responses
   STANDARD: CASAS 4.1.5
   OPD TERM: dress appropriately

8. **ANSWER:** A
   REFERENCE: OPD, Interview Skills, p. 174
   OBJECTIVE: Follow procedures for applying for a job, including interpreting and completing job applications, resumes, and letters of application
   STANDARD: CASAS 4.1.2
   OPD TERM: bring your resume and ID

9. **ANSWER:** A
   REFERENCE: OPD, Interview Skills, p. 174
   OBJECTIVE: Identify procedures involved in interviewing for a job, such as arranging for an interview, acting and dressing appropriately, and selecting appropriate questions and responses
   STANDARD: CASAS 4.1.5
   OPD TERM: be neat

10. **ANSWER:** shake hands
    REFERENCE: OPD, Interview Skills, p. 174
    OBJECTIVE: Identify appropriate behavior and attitudes for getting a job
    STANDARD: CASAS 4.1.7
    OPD TERM: shake hands

Job Safety, pp. 87–88

1. **ANSWER:** F
   REFERENCE: OPD, Job Safety, p. 179
   OBJECTIVE: Identify safe work procedures and common safety equipment, including wearing safe work attire
   STANDARD: CASAS 4.3.3
   OPD TERM: frayed cord

2. **ANSWER:** T
   REFERENCE: OPD, Job Safety, p. 179
   OBJECTIVE: Identify safe work procedures and common safety equipment, including wearing safe work attire
   STANDARD: CASAS 4.3.3
   OPD TERM: broken equipment

3. **ANSWER:** C
   REFERENCE: OPD, Job Safety, p. 179
   OBJECTIVE: Make comparisons, differentiating among, sorting, and classifying items, information, or ideas
   STANDARD: CASAS 7.2.3
   OPD TERM: careful worker

4. **ANSWER:** D
   REFERENCE: OPD, Job Safety, p. 179
   OBJECTIVE: Make comparisons, differentiating among, sorting, and classifying items, information, or ideas
   STANDARD: CASAS 7.2.3
   OPD TERM: knee pads

5. **ANSWER:** D
   REFERENCE: OPD, Job Safety, p. 179
   OBJECTIVE: Identify safe work procedures and common safety equipment, including wearing safe work attire
   STANDARD: CASAS 4.3.3
   OPD TERM: ear plugs

6. **ANSWER:** A
   REFERENCE: OPD, Job Safety, p. 179
   OBJECTIVE: Interpret work safety manuals and related information
   STANDARD: CASAS 4.3.2
   OPD TERM: slippery floor

7. **ANSWER:** B
   REFERENCE: OPD, Job Safety, p. 179
   OBJECTIVE: Identify safe work procedures and common safety equipment, including wearing safe work attire
   STANDARD: CASAS 4.3.3
   OPD TERM: careless worker

8. **ANSWER:** B
   REFERENCE: OPD, Job Safety, p. 179
   OBJECTIVE: Identify safe work procedures and common safety equipment, including wearing safe work attire
   STANDARD: CASAS 4.3.3
   OPD TERM: safety boots

9. **ANSWER:** C
   REFERENCE: OPD, Job Safety, p. 179
   OBJECTIVE: Identify safe work procedures and common safety equipment, including wearing safe work attire
   STANDARD: CASAS 4.3.3
   OPD TERM: fire extinguisher

10. **ANSWER:** safety goggles
    REFERENCE: OPD, Job Safety, p. 179
    OBJECTIVE: Identify safe work procedures and common safety equipment, including wearing safe work attire
    STANDARD: CASAS 4.3.3
    OPD TERM: safety goggles

An Office, pp. 89–90

1. **ANSWER:** F
   REFERENCE: OPD, An Office, pp. 182–183
   OBJECTIVE: Identify common tools, equipment, machines, and materials required for one's job
   STANDARD: CASAS 4.5.1
   OPD TERM: scanner

2. **ANSWER:** F
   REFERENCE: OPD, An Office, pp. 182–183
   OBJECTIVE: Identify common tools, equipment, machines, and materials required for one's job
   STANDARD: CASAS 4.5.1
   OPD TERM: stapler

3. **ANSWER:** T
   REFERENCE: OPD, An Office, pp. 182–183
   OBJECTIVE: Demonstrate ability to select, set up and use tools and machines in order to accomplish a task, while operating within a technological system
   STANDARD: CASAS 4.5.6
   OPD TERM: laser printer

4. **ANSWER:** D
REFERENCE: OPD, An Office, pp. 182–183
OBJECTIVE: Demonstrate ability to use a filing system or other ordered system
STANDARD: CASAS 4.5.3
OPD TERM: file cabinet

5. **ANSWER:** D
REFERENCE: OPD, An Office, pp. 182–183
OBJECTIVE: Interpret general work-related vocabulary (e.g., experience, swing shift)
STANDARD: CASAS 4.1.6
OPD TERM: cubicle

6. **ANSWER:** A
REFERENCE: OPD, An Office, pp. 182–183
OBJECTIVE: Identify common tools, equipment, machines, and materials required for one's job
STANDARD: CASAS 4.5.1
OPD TERM: paper clip

7. **ANSWER:** C
REFERENCE: OPD, An Office, pp. 182–183
OBJECTIVE: Identify common occupations and the skills and education required for them
STANDARD: CASAS 4.1.8
OPD TERM: computer technician

8. **ANSWER:** B
REFERENCE: OPD, An Office, pp. 182–183
OBJECTIVE: Interpret general work-related vocabulary (e.g., experience, swing shift)
STANDARD: CASAS 4.1.6
OPD TERM: conference room

9. **ANSWER:** A
REFERENCE: OPD, An Office, pp. 182–183
OBJECTIVE: Interpret general work-related vocabulary (e.g., experience, swing shift)
STANDARD: CASAS 4.1.6
OPD TERM: supply cabinet

10. **ANSWER:** photocopier
REFERENCE: OPD, An Office, pp. 182–183
OBJECTIVE: Demonstrate use of common business machines
STANDARD: CASAS 4.5.4
OPD TERM: photocopier

A Hotel, pp. 91–92

1. **ANSWER:** T
REFERENCE: OPD, A Hotel, p. 184
OBJECTIVE: Identify common occupations and the skills and education required for them
STANDARD: CASAS 4.1.8
OPD TERM: doorman

2. **ANSWER:** F
REFERENCE: OPD, A Hotel, p. 184
OBJECTIVE: Identify common occupations and the skills and education required for them
STANDARD: CASAS 4.1.8
OPD TERM: concierge

3. **ANSWER:** D
REFERENCE: OPD, A Hotel, p. 184
OBJECTIVE: Identify common occupations and the skills and education required for them
STANDARD: CASAS 4.1.8
OPD TERM: bellhop

4. **ANSWER:** D
REFERENCE: OPD, A Hotel, p. 184
OBJECTIVE: Interpret information about recreational and entertainment facilities and activities
STANDARD: CASAS 2.6.1
OPD TERM: front desk

5. **ANSWER:** C
REFERENCE: OPD, A Hotel, p. 184
OBJECTIVE: Identify common occupations and the skills and education required for them
STANDARD: CASAS 4.1.8
OPD TERM: housekeeper

6. **ANSWER:** A
REFERENCE: OPD, A Hotel, p. 184
OBJECTIVE: Interpret information about recreational and entertainment facilities and activities
STANDARD: CASAS 2.6.1
OPD TERM: guest room

7. **ANSWER:** C
REFERENCE: OPD, A Hotel, p. 184
OBJECTIVE: Identify common occupations and the skills and education required for them
STANDARD: CASAS 4.1.8
OPD TERM: parking attendant

8. **ANSWER:** D
REFERENCE: OPD, A Hotel, p. 184
OBJECTIVE: Identify common occupations and the skills and education required for them
STANDARD: CASAS 4.1.8
OPD TERM: desk clerk

9. **ANSWER:** B
REFERENCE: OPD, A Hotel, p. 184
OBJECTIVE: Demonstrate effective communication skills in working with customers and clients
STANDARD: CASAS 4.8.3
OPD TERM: luggage cart

10. **ANSWER:** B
REFERENCE: OPD, A Hotel, p. 184
OBJECTIVE: Interpret information about recreational and entertainment facilities and activities
STANDARD: CASAS 2.6.1
OPD TERM: room service

English Composition, pp. 93–94

1. **ANSWER:** T
REFERENCE: OPD, English Composition, pp. 190–191
OBJECTIVE: Evaluate a situation, statement, or process, assembling information and providing evidence, making judgments, examining assumptions, and identifying contradictions
STANDARD: CASAS 7.2.5
OPD TERM: paragraph

2. **ANSWER:** F
REFERENCE: OPD, English Composition, pp. 190–191
OBJECTIVE: Evaluate a situation, statement, or process, assembling information and providing evidence, making judgments, examining assumptions, and identifying contradictions
STANDARD: CASAS 7.2.5
OPD TERM: final draft

3. **ANSWER:** C
REFERENCE: OPD, English Composition, pp. 190–191
OBJECTIVE: Identify or make inferences through inductive and deductive reasoning to hypothesize, predict, conclude, and synthesize; distinguish fact from opinion, and determine what is mandatory and what is discretionary
STANDARD: CASAS 7.2.4
OPD TERM: comma

4. **ANSWER:** A
REFERENCE: OPD, English Composition, pp. 190–191
OBJECTIVE: Identify or make inferences through inductive and deductive reasoning to hypothesize, predict, conclude, and synthesize; distinguish fact from opinion, and determine what is mandatory and what is discretionary
STANDARD: CASAS 7.2.4
OPD TERM: sentence

5. **ANSWER:** B
REFERENCE: OPD, English Composition, pp. 190–191
OBJECTIVE: Identify or make inferences through inductive and deductive reasoning to hypothesize, predict, conclude, and synthesize; distinguish fact from opinion, and determine what is mandatory and what is discretionary
STANDARD: CASAS 7.2.4
OPD TERM: edit

6. **ANSWER:** A
REFERENCE: OPD, English Composition, pp. 190–191
OBJECTIVE: Identify or make inferences through inductive and deductive reasoning to hypothesize, predict, conclude, and synthesize; distinguish fact from opinion, and determine what is mandatory and what is discretionary
STANDARD: CASAS 7.2.4
OPD TERM: exclamation mark

7. **ANSWER:** D
REFERENCE: OPD, English Composition, pp. 190–191
OBJECTIVE: Identify or make inferences through inductive and deductive reasoning to hypothesize, predict, conclude, and synthesize; distinguish fact from opinion, and determine what is mandatory and what is discretionary
STANDARD: CASAS 7.2.4
OPD TERM: period

8. **ANSWER:** C
REFERENCE: OPD, English Composition, pp. 190–191
OBJECTIVE: Identify or make inferences through inductive and deductive reasoning to hypothesize, predict, conclude, and synthesize; distinguish fact from opinion, and determine what is mandatory and what is discretionary
STANDARD: CASAS 7.2.4
OPD TERM: write a first draft

9. **ANSWER:** B
REFERENCE: OPD, English Composition, pp. 190–191
OBJECTIVE: Identify or make inferences through inductive and deductive reasoning to hypothesize, predict, conclude, and synthesize; distinguish fact from opinion, and determine what is mandatory and what is discretionary
STANDARD: CASAS 7.2.4
OPD TERM: apostrophe

10. **ANSWER:** quotation marks
REFERENCE: OPD, English Composition, pp. 190–191
OBJECTIVE: Identify or make inferences through inductive and deductive reasoning to hypothesize, predict, conclude, and synthesize; distinguish fact from opinion, and determine what is mandatory and what is discretionary
STANDARD: CASAS 7.2.4
OPD TERM: quotation marks

Science, pp. 95–96

1. **ANSWER:** F
   REFERENCE: OPD, Science, pp. 194–195
   OBJECTIVE: Evaluate a situation, statement, or process, assembling information and providing evidence, making judgments, examining assumptions, and identifying contradictions
   STANDARD: CASAS 7.2.5
   OPD TERM: chemist

2. **ANSWER:** F
   REFERENCE: OPD, Science, pp. 194–195
   OBJECTIVE: Make comparisons, differentiating among, sorting, and classifying items, information, or ideas
   STANDARD: CASAS 7.2.3
   OPD TERM: atom

3. **ANSWER:** T
   REFERENCE: OPD, Science, pp. 194–195
   OBJECTIVE: Evaluate a situation, statement, or process, assembling information and providing evidence, making judgments, examining assumptions, and identifying contradictions
   STANDARD: CASAS 7.2.5
   OPD TERM: test tube

4. **ANSWER:** F
   REFERENCE: OPD, Science, pp. 194–195
   OBJECTIVE: Make comparisons, differentiating among, sorting, and classifying items, information, or ideas
   STANDARD: CASAS 7.2.3
   OPD TERM: molecule

5. **ANSWER:** F
   REFERENCE: OPD, Science, pp. 194–195
   OBJECTIVE: Make comparisons, differentiating among, sorting, and classifying items, information, or ideas
   STANDARD: CASAS 7.2.3
   OPD TERM: organisms

6. **ANSWER:** T
   REFERENCE: OPD, Science, pp. 194–195
   OBJECTIVE: Make comparisons, differentiating among, sorting, and classifying items, information, or ideas
   STANDARD: CASAS 7.2.3
   OPD TERM: cell

7. **ANSWER:** C
   REFERENCE: OPD, Science, pp. 194–195
   OBJECTIVE: Identify or make inferences through inductive and deductive reasoning to hypothesize, predict, conclude, and synthesize; distinguish fact from opinion, and determine what is mandatory and what is discretionary
   STANDARD: CASAS 7.2.4
   OPD TERM: biologist

8. **ANSWER:** D
   REFERENCE: OPD, Science, pp. 194–195
   OBJECTIVE: Identify or make inferences through inductive and deductive reasoning to hypothesize, predict, conclude, and synthesize; distinguish fact from opinion, and determine what is mandatory and what is discretionary
   STANDARD: CASAS 7.2.4
   OPD TERM: eyepiece

9. **ANSWER:** C
   REFERENCE: OPD, Science, pp. 194–195
   OBJECTIVE: Identify or make inferences through inductive and deductive reasoning to hypothesize, predict, conclude, and synthesize; distinguish fact from opinion, and determine what is mandatory and what is discretionary
   STANDARD: CASAS 7.2.4
   OPD TERM: beaker

10. **ANSWER:** A
    REFERENCE: OPD, Science, pp. 194–195
    OBJECTIVE: Identify or make inferences through inductive and deductive reasoning to hypothesize, predict, conclude, and synthesize; distinguish fact from opinion, and determine what is mandatory and what is discretionary
    STANDARD: CASAS 7.2.4
    OPD TERM: Bunsen burner

11. **ANSWER:** B
    REFERENCE: OPD, Science, pp. 194–195
    OBJECTIVE: Identify or make inferences through inductive and deductive reasoning to hypothesize, predict, conclude, and synthesize; distinguish fact from opinion, and determine what is mandatory and what is discretionary
    STANDARD: CASAS 7.2.4
    OPD TERM: arm

12. **ANSWER:** A
    REFERENCE: OPD, Science, pp. 194–195
    OBJECTIVE: Analyze a situation, statement, or process, identifying component elements and causal and part/whole relationships
    STANDARD: CASAS 7.2.2
    OPD TERM: stage

13. **ANSWER:** B
    REFERENCE: OPD, Science, pp. 194–195
    OBJECTIVE: Identify or make inferences through inductive and deductive reasoning to hypothesize, predict, conclude, and synthesize; distinguish fact from opinion, and determine what is mandatory and what is discretionary
    STANDARD: CASAS 7.2.4
    OPD TERM: periodic table

14. **ANSWER:** B
    REFERENCE: OPD, Science, pp. 194–195
    OBJECTIVE: Demonstrate an organized approach to achieving goals, including identifying and prioritizing tasks and setting and following an effective schedule
    STANDARD: CASAS 7.1.2
    OPD TERM: slide

15. **ANSWER:** nucleus
    REFERENCE: OPD, Science, pp. 194–195
    OBJECTIVE: Identify or use appropriate language for informational purposes;
    STANDARD: CASAS 0.1.2
    OPD TERM: nucleus

Computers, pp. 97–98

1. **ANSWER:** T
   REFERENCE: OPD, Computers, p. 196
   OBJECTIVE: Demonstrate basic computer skills and use of common software programs, including reading or interpreting computer-generated printouts
   STANDARD: CASAS 4.5.5
   OPD TERM: hard drive

2. **ANSWER:** T
   REFERENCE: OPD, Computers, p. 196
   OBJECTIVE: Demonstrate basic computer skills and use of common software programs, including reading or interpreting computer-generated printouts
   STANDARD: CASAS 4.5.5
   OPD TERM: delete

3. **ANSWER:** B
   REFERENCE: OPD, Computers, p. 196
   OBJECTIVE: Demonstrate basic computer skills and use of common software programs, including reading or interpreting computer-generated printouts
   STANDARD: CASAS 4.5.5
   OPD TERM: printer

4. **ANSWER:** C
   REFERENCE: OPD, Computers, p. 196
   OBJECTIVE: Demonstrate basic computer skills and use of common software programs, including reading or interpreting computer-generated printouts
   STANDARD: CASAS 4.5.5
   OPD TERM: tower

5. **ANSWER:** D
   REFERENCE: OPD, Computers, p. 196
   OBJECTIVE: Demonstrate basic computer skills and use of common software programs, including reading or interpreting computer-generated printouts
   STANDARD: CASAS 4.5.5
   OPD TERM: software

6. **ANSWER:** C
   REFERENCE: OPD, Computers, p. 196
   OBJECTIVE: Demonstrate basic computer skills and use of common software programs, including reading or interpreting computer-generated printouts
   STANDARD: CASAS 4.5.5
   OPD TERM: DVD and CD-ROM drive

7. **ANSWER:** D
   REFERENCE: OPD, Computers, p. 196
   OBJECTIVE: Demonstrate basic computer skills and use of common software programs, including reading or interpreting computer-generated printouts
   STANDARD: CASAS 4.5.5
   OPD TERM: mouse

8. **ANSWER:** A
   REFERENCE: OPD, Computers, p. 196
   OBJECTIVE: Demonstrate basic computer skills and use of common software programs, including reading or interpreting computer-generated printouts
   STANDARD: CASAS 4.5.5
   OPD TERM: monitor

9. **ANSWER:** B
   REFERENCE: OPD, Computers, p. 196
   OBJECTIVE: Demonstrate simple keyboarding skills
   STANDARD: CASAS 4.5.2
   OPD TERM: select

10. **ANSWER:** keyboard
    REFERENCE: OPD, Computers, p. 196
    OBJECTIVE: Demonstrate simple keyboarding skills
    STANDARD: CASAS 4.5.2
    OPD TERM: keyboard

The Internet, pp. 99–100

1. **ANSWER:** T
   REFERENCE: OPD, The Internet, p. 197
   OBJECTIVE: Demonstrate basic computer skills and use of common software programs, including reading or interpreting computer-generated printouts
   STANDARD: CASAS 4.5.5
   OPD TERM: pointer

2. **ANSWER:** F
   REFERENCE: OPD, The Internet, p. 197
   OBJECTIVE: Demonstrate basic computer skills and use of common software programs, including reading or interpreting computer-generated printouts
   STANDARD: CASAS 4.5.5
   OPD TERM: back button

3. **ANSWER:** T
   REFERENCE: OPD, The Internet, p. 197
   OBJECTIVE: Demonstrate basic computer skills and use of common software programs, including reading or interpreting computer-generated printouts
   STANDARD: CASAS 4.5.5
   OPD TERM: menu bar

4. **ANSWER:** D
   REFERENCE: OPD, The Internet, p. 197
   OBJECTIVE: Identify or utilize appropriate informational resources, including the Internet
   STANDARD: CASAS 7.4.4
   OPD TERM: scroll bar

5. **ANSWER:** A
   REFERENCE: OPD, The Internet, p. 197
   OBJECTIVE: Demonstrate basic computer skills and use of common software programs, including reading or interpreting computer-generated printouts
   STANDARD: CASAS 4.5.5
   OPD TERM: send the email

6. **ANSWER:** B
   REFERENCE: OPD, The Internet, p. 197
   OBJECTIVE: Identify or utilize appropriate informational resources, including the Internet
   STANDARD: CASAS 7.4.4
   OPD TERM: type the message

7. **ANSWER:** A
   REFERENCE: OPD, The Internet, p. 197
   OBJECTIVE: Demonstrate basic computer skills and use of common software programs, including reading or interpreting computer-generated printouts
   STANDARD: CASAS 4.5.5
   OPD TERM: cursor

8. **ANSWER:** B
   REFERENCE: OPD, The Internet, p. 197
   OBJECTIVE: Demonstrate basic computer skills and use of common software programs, including reading or interpreting computer-generated printouts
   STANDARD: CASAS 4.5.5
   OPD TERM: address the email

9. **ANSWER:** C
   REFERENCE: OPD, The Internet, p. 197
   OBJECTIVE: Identify or utilize appropriate informational resources, including the Internet
   STANDARD: CASAS 7.4.4
   OPD TERM: URL

10. **ANSWER:** A
    REFERENCE: OPD, The Internet, p. 197
    OBJECTIVE: Demonstrate basic computer skills and use of common software programs, including reading or interpreting computer-generated printouts
    STANDARD: CASAS 4.5.5
    OPD TERM: click "sign in"

U.S. History, pp. 101–102

1. **ANSWER:** F
   REFERENCE: OPD, U.S. History, p. 198
   OBJECTIVE: Interpret information about U.S. history
   STANDARD: CASAS 5.2.1
   OPD TERM: Native Americans

2. **ANSWER:** F
   REFERENCE: OPD, U.S. History, p. 198
   OBJECTIVE: Identify or interpret U.S. historical documents
   STANDARD: CASAS 5.2.2
   OPD TERM: Bill of Rights

3. **ANSWER:** T
   REFERENCE: OPD, U.S. History, p. 198
   OBJECTIVE: Interpret information about U.S. history
   STANDARD: CASAS 5.2.1
   OPD TERM: Revolutionary War

4. **ANSWER:** T
   REFERENCE: OPD, U.S. History, p. 198
   OBJECTIVE: Interpret information about U.S. history
   STANDARD: CASAS 5.2.1
   OPD TERM: slave

5. **ANSWER:** F
   REFERENCE: OPD, U.S. History, p. 198
   OBJECTIVE: Interpret information about U.S. history
   STANDARD: CASAS 5.2.1
   OPD TERM: colonists

6. **ANSWER:** D
   REFERENCE: OPD, U.S. History, p. 198
   OBJECTIVE: Identify or interpret U.S. historical documents
   STANDARD: CASAS 5.2.2
   OPD TERM: Constitution

7. **ANSWER:** A
   REFERENCE: OPD, U.S. History, p. 198
   OBJECTIVE: Interpret information about U.S. history
   STANDARD: CASAS 5.2.1
   OPD TERM: founders

8. **ANSWER:** D
   REFERENCE: OPD, U.S. History, p. 198
   OBJECTIVE: Identify or interpret U.S. historical documents
   STANDARD: CASAS 5.2.2
   OPD TERM: Declaration of Independence

9. **ANSWER:** A
   REFERENCE: OPD, U.S. History, p. 198
   OBJECTIVE: Interpret information about U.S. history
   STANDARD: CASAS 5.2.1
   OPD TERM: first president

10. **ANSWER:** A
    REFERENCE: OPD, U.S. History, p. 198
    OBJECTIVE: Interpret information about U.S. history
    STANDARD: CASAS 5.2.1
    OPD TERM: thirteen colonies

Energy and Conservation, pp. 103–104

1. **ANSWER:** T
   REFERENCE: OPD, Energy and Conservation, pp. 218–219
   OBJECTIVE: Interpret information related to physics, including energy
   STANDARD: CASAS 5.7.2
   OPD TERM: solar energy

2. **ANSWER:** F
   REFERENCE: OPD, Energy and Conservation, pp. 218–219
   OBJECTIVE: Interpret information related to physics, including energy
   STANDARD: CASAS 5.7.2
   OPD TERM: natural gas

3. **ANSWER:** F
   REFERENCE: OPD, Energy and Conservation, pp. 218–219
   OBJECTIVE: Interpret information related to physics, including energy
   STANDARD: CASAS 5.7.2
   OPD TERM: nuclear energy

4. **ANSWER:** T
   REFERENCE: OPD, Energy and Conservation, pp. 218–219
   OBJECTIVE: Interpret information related to physics, including energy
   STANDARD: CASAS 5.7.2
   OPD TERM: wind power

5. **ANSWER:** T
   REFERENCE: OPD, Energy and Conservation, pp. 218–219
   OBJECTIVE: Interpret information about environmental issues
   STANDARD: CASAS 5.7.1
   OPD TERM: carpool

6. **ANSWER:** B
   REFERENCE: OPD, Energy and Conservation, pp. 218–219
   OBJECTIVE: Interpret information about environmental issues
   STANDARD: CASAS 5.7.1
   OPD TERM: air pollution

7. **ANSWER:** B
   REFERENCE: OPD, Energy and Conservation, pp. 218–219
   OBJECTIVE: Interpret information related to physics, including energy
   STANDARD: CASAS 5.7.2
   OPD TERM: hazardous waste

8. **ANSWER:** C
   REFERENCE: OPD, Energy and Conservation, pp. 218–219
   OBJECTIVE: Interpret information related to physics, including energy
   STANDARD: CASAS 5.7.2
   OPD TERM: oil

9. **ANSWER:** D
   REFERENCE: OPD, Energy and Conservation, pp. 218–219
   OBJECTIVE: Interpret information related to physics, including energy
   STANDARD: CASAS 5.7.2
   OPD TERM: coal

10. **ANSWER:** C
    REFERENCE: OPD, Energy and Conservation, pp. 218–219
    OBJECTIVE: Interpret information about environmental issues
    STANDARD: CASAS 5.7.1
    OPD TERM: turn off lights

11. **ANSWER:** D
    REFERENCE: OPD, Energy and Conservation, pp. 218–219
    OBJECTIVE: Interpret information about environmental issues
    STANDARD: CASAS 5.7.1
    OPD TERM: don't litter

12. **ANSWER:** A
    REFERENCE: OPD, Energy and Conservation, pp. 218–219
    OBJECTIVE: Interpret information about environmental issues
    STANDARD: CASAS 5.7.1
    OPD TERM: water pollution

13. **ANSWER:** C
    REFERENCE: OPD, Energy and Conservation, pp. 218–219
    OBJECTIVE: Interpret information about environmental issues
    STANDARD: CASAS 5.7.1
    OPD TERM: save water

14. **ANSWER:** D
REFERENCE: OPD, Energy and Conservation, pp. 218–219
OBJECTIVE: Interpret information about environmental issues
STANDARD: CASAS 5.7.1
OPD TERM: recycle

15. **ANSWER:** C
REFERENCE: OPD, Energy and Conservation, pp. 218–219
OBJECTIVE: Interpret information related to physics, including energy
STANDARD: CASAS 5.7.2
OPD TERM: reduce trash

Places to Go, pp. 105–106

1. **ANSWER:** T
REFERENCE: OPD, Places to Go, pp. 222–223
OBJECTIVE: Interpret information about recreational and entertainment facilities and activities
STANDARD: CASAS 2.6.1
OPD TERM: zoo

2. **ANSWER:** F
REFERENCE: OPD, Places to Go, pp. 222–223
OBJECTIVE: Interpret materials related to the arts, such as fine art, music, drama, and film
STANDARD: CASAS 2.7.6
OPD TERM: classical concert

3. **ANSWER:** A
REFERENCE: OPD, Places to Go, pp. 222–223
OBJECTIVE: Interpret materials related to the arts, such as fine art, music, drama, and film
STANDARD: CASAS 2.7.6
OPD TERM: art museum

4. **ANSWER:** D
REFERENCE: OPD, Places to Go, pp. 222–223
OBJECTIVE: Interpret information about recreational and entertainment facilities and activities
STANDARD: CASAS 2.6.1
OPD TERM: aquarium

5. **ANSWER:** D
REFERENCE: OPD, Places to Go, pp. 222–223
OBJECTIVE: Interpret information about recreational and entertainment facilities and activities
STANDARD: CASAS 2.6.1
OPD TERM: county fair

6. **ANSWER:** A
REFERENCE: OPD, Places to Go, pp. 222–223
OBJECTIVE: Interpret information about recreational and entertainment facilities and activities
STANDARD: CASAS 2.6.1
OPD TERM: botanical garden

7. **ANSWER:** B
REFERENCE: OPD, Places to Go, pp. 222–223
OBJECTIVE: Interpret materials related to the arts, such as fine art, music, drama, and film
STANDARD: CASAS 2.7.6
OPD TERM: play

8. **ANSWER:** C
REFERENCE: OPD, Places to Go, pp. 222–223
OBJECTIVE: Interpret information about recreational and entertainment facilities and activities
STANDARD: CASAS 2.6.1
OPD TERM: bowling alley

9. **ANSWER:** D
REFERENCE: OPD, Places to Go, pp. 222–223
OBJECTIVE: Interpret materials related to the arts, such as fine art, music, drama, and film
STANDARD: CASAS 2.7.6
OPD TERM: opera

10. **ANSWER:** amusement park
REFERENCE: OPD, Places to Go, pp. 222–223
OBJECTIVE: Interpret information about recreational and entertainment facilities and activities
STANDARD: CASAS 2.6.1
OPD TERM: amusement park

Entertainment, pp. 107–108

1. **ANSWER:** F
REFERENCE: OPD, Entertainment, pp. 236–237
OBJECTIVE: Locate information in TV, movie, and other recreational listings
STANDARD: CASAS 2.6.2
OPD TERM: soap opera

2. **ANSWER:** T
REFERENCE: OPD, Entertainment, pp. 236–237
OBJECTIVE: Interpret materials related to the arts, such as fine art, music, drama, and film
STANDARD: CASAS 2.7.6
OPD TERM: drama

3. **ANSWER:** A
REFERENCE: OPD, Entertainment, pp. 236–237
OBJECTIVE: Locate information in TV, movie, and other recreational listings
STANDARD: CASAS 2.6.2
OPD TERM: sitcom (situation comedy)

4. **ANSWER:** D
REFERENCE: OPD, Entertainment, pp. 236–237
OBJECTIVE: Locate information in TV, movie, and other recreational listings
STANDARD: CASAS 2.6.2
OPD TERM: news program

5. **ANSWER:** D
REFERENCE: OPD, Entertainment, pp. 236–237
OBJECTIVE: Interpret materials related to the arts, such as fine art, music, drama, and film
STANDARD: CASAS 2.7.6
OPD TERM: action story

6. **ANSWER:** D
REFERENCE: OPD, Entertainment, pp. 236–237
OBJECTIVE: Locate information in TV, movie, and other recreational listings
STANDARD: CASAS 2.6.2
OPD TERM: reality show

7. **ANSWER:** A
REFERENCE: OPD, Entertainment, pp. 236–237
OBJECTIVE: Locate information in TV, movie, and other recreational listings
STANDARD: CASAS 2.6.2
OPD TERM: mystery

8. **ANSWER:** D
REFERENCE: OPD, Entertainment, pp. 236–237
OBJECTIVE: Converse about daily and leisure activities and personal interests
STANDARD: CASAS 0.2.4
OPD TERM: sports program

9. **ANSWER:** C
REFERENCE: OPD, Entertainment, pp. 236–237
OBJECTIVE: Converse about daily and leisure activities and personal interests
STANDARD: CASAS 0.2.4
OPD TERM: pop

10. **ANSWER:** Soul
REFERENCE: OPD, Entertainment, pp. 236–237
OBJECTIVE: Interpret materials related to the arts, such as fine art, music, drama, and film
STANDARD: CASAS 2.7.6
OPD TERM: soul

Holidays, pp. 109–110

1. **ANSWER:** A
REFERENCE: OPD, Holidays, p. 239
OBJECTIVE: Interpret information about holidays
STANDARD: CASAS 2.7.1
OPD TERM: jack-o'-lantern

2. **ANSWER:** B
REFERENCE: OPD, Holidays, p. 239
OBJECTIVE: Interpret materials related to the arts, such as fine art, music, drama, and film
STANDARD: CASAS 2.7.1
OPD TERM: mask

3. **ANSWER:** D
REFERENCE: OPD, Holidays, p. 239
OBJECTIVE: Interpret information about holidays
STANDARD: CASAS 2.7.1
OPD TERM: parade

4. **ANSWER:** D
REFERENCE: OPD, Holidays, p. 239
OBJECTIVE: Interpret information about holidays
STANDARD: CASAS 2.7.1
OPD TERM: feast

5. **ANSWER:** C
REFERENCE: OPD, Holidays, p. 239
OBJECTIVE: Interpret information about holidays
STANDARD: CASAS 2.7.1
OPD TERM: costume

6. **ANSWER:** D
REFERENCE: OPD, Holidays, p. 239
OBJECTIVE: Interpret information about holidays
STANDARD: CASAS 2.7.1
OPD TERM: flag

7. **ANSWER:** C
REFERENCE: OPD, Holidays, p. 239
OBJECTIVE: Interpret information about holidays
STANDARD: CASAS 2.7.1
OPD TERM: Christmas tree

8. **ANSWER:** A
REFERENCE: OPD, Holidays, p. 239
OBJECTIVE: Interpret information about holidays
STANDARD: CASAS 2.7.1
OPD TERM: fireworks

9. **ANSWER:** C
REFERENCE: OPD, Holidays, p. 239
OBJECTIVE: Converse about daily and leisure activities and personal interests
STANDARD: CASAS 0.2.4
OPD TERM: float

10. **ANSWER:** D
REFERENCE: OPD, Holidays, p. 239
OBJECTIVE: Converse about daily and leisure activities and personal interests
STANDARD: CASAS 0.2.4
OPD TERM: ornament